D0055683

Praise for
*Unlock Your Dream*

"Everybody has a dream, but few know how to make it a reality. Let Philip Wagner be your guide! He's a man who can help get you where you want to be, because he knows how to trust God for the impossible."

—RICK WARREN, pastor of Saddleback Church and *New York Times* best-selling author of *The Purpose Driven Life*

"Philip Wagner has been a friend of mine for a long time. I like a lot of things about him, but right at the top of the list is that he's a dreamer. Dreams can be brain-candy that take us away from the present, but the best dreams are the ones that launch us into the future. This book is a conversation with a trusted friend about what could happen if we traded in our small-sized dreams and ambitions for some of the big ones Jesus talked about."

—BOB GOFF, *New York Times* best-selling author of *Love Does;* founder of *Love Does,* a nonprofit human rights organization; and Honorary Consul for the Republic of Uganda to the United States

"Everyone dreams. As we get older, realities of life adjust our dreams, usually downsizing them. In *Unlock Your Dream,* my friend Philip Wagner reignites the dream, helps us understand why we have rationalized our dreams away, and gives us pragmatic steps to dream once again."

—SAM CHAND, leadership consultant and author of *Leadership Pain*

"So many of my God-dreams have been realized because I have applied Philip Wagner's teachings to my life. Reading his wise words in *Unlock Your Dream* on surviving through hurt and betrayals has been a soothing balm to my soul. I am excited for you to unleash the power of your God-dreams, the same way Philip has, with God's hand, shown me."

—SHERRI SHEPHERD, former cohost of *The View* and star of NBC's *Trial and Error*

"We all have difficulties in figuring out what our purpose is on this earth. Philip Wagner has found a way for us to whittle away the parts of our dreams that are selfish and focus on the dreams that are God-centered. If you are looking for God to use your life for His glory and to have a great and fulfilling time along the way, this book is for you!"

—BARRY ZITO, Cy Young Award–winning pitcher and three-time
  All-Star for the Oakland A's

"We all dream of a life that matters. We have a desire to make a real difference but often don't know how. In *Unlock Your Dream,* Philip Wagner will inspire you to push past your doubts and give you the confidence you need to reach your God-dream."

—CRAIG GROESCHEL, pastor of Life.Church and *New York
  Times* best-selling author of *#Struggles: Following Jesus
  in a Selfie-Centered World*

"*Unlock Your Dream* breathes new life into that stirring in your heart you so desperately want to pursue. Philip identifies the challenges we'll face in launching our God-given dreams while also providing the encouragement we need to keep moving forward."

—LYSA TERKEURST, *New York Times* best-selling author
  and president of Proverbs 31 Ministries

"I believe the Holy Spirit has sovereignly ordered the steps of your life to the intersection of Pastor Philip Wagner. In his book, *Unlock Your Dream,* Philip humbly reveals the divine purpose and destiny assigned to his life: 'It's part of my dream to release you so you can reach your dreams too.' Through practical vignettes of dreams, dreamers, and dream-makers, every page both pushes and calls you to dream and dream big!"

—BISHOP KENNETH C. ULMER, DMin, PhD, Faithful Central Bible
  Church and former president of the King's University, Los Angeles

"*Unlock Your Dream* will not only encourage those who read it to remain faithful to their dream, but it will also provide insight about how to do it."

—AL KASHA, two-time Academy Award–winning songwriter and composer

"Not many people you'll meet will be as genuinely inspiring as Philip Wagner. He's lived an extraordinary life as a husband, dad, and pastor—and now he's penned a practical but personal guidebook for us to reach our highest God-given dreams along the real and sometimes rocky roads of life. He's a modern-day happy sage with stories to tell and wisdom to share."

—JUDAH SMITH, lead pastor of the City Church and *New York Times* best-selling author of *Jesus Is_____* .

"Culture has always been created and grown through dreamers who dare to dream big. In Philip Wagner's book *Unlock Your Dream,* you will discover that setbacks and past hurts don't have to keep you from the dream God has put in your heart. Philip is honest and transparent about the challenges he has faced and gives us a glimpse into his personal journey, which will encourage and inspire you to dream again."

—DARLENE ZSCHECH

"Dreams are your view of the future. Dreams are the substance of great achievement. In his new book, Philip Wagner shares the events in his life that taught him how to unlock his dreams and face the future with anticipation and excitement instead of hopelessness and apprehension. It will change your life!"

—A. R. BERNARD, founder, senior pastor, and CEO of Christian Cultural Center in Brooklyn, New York

# UNLOCK YOUR DREAM

## DISCOVER THE ADVENTURE
## YOU WERE CREATED FOR

# PHILIP WAGNER

**WATERBROOK**

Unlock Your Dream

All Scripture quotations, unless otherwise indicated, are taken from the Holy Bible, New International Version®, NIV®. Copyright © 1973, 1978, 1984, 2011 by Biblica Inc.® Used by permission. All rights reserved worldwide. Scripture quotations marked (AMPC) are taken from the Amplified Bible Classic Edition. Copyright © 1954, 1958, 1962, 1964, 1965, 1987 by the Lockman Foundation. Used by permission. (www. Lockman.org). Scripture quotations marked (CEV) are taken from the Contemporary English Version. Copyright © 1991, 1992, 1995 by American Bible Society. Used by permission. Scripture quotations marked (ESV) are taken from the ESV® Bible (the Holy Bible, English Standard Version®), copyright © 2001 by Crossway, a publishing ministry of Good News Publishers. Used by permission. All rights reserved. Scripture quotations marked (MSG) are taken from The Message. Copyright © by Eugene H. Peterson 1993, 1994, 1995, 1996, 2000, 2001, 2002. Used by permission of Tyndale House Publishers Inc. Scripture quotations marked (NKJV) are taken from the New King James Version®. Copyright © 1982 by Thomas Nelson Inc. Used by permission. All rights reserved. Scripture quotations marked (NLT) are taken from the Holy Bible, New Living Translation, copyright © 1996, 2004, 2007, 2013, 2015 by Tyndale House Foundation. Used by permission of Tyndale House Publishers Inc., Carol Stream, Illinois 60188. All rights reserved.

Italics in Scripture quotations reflect the author's added emphasis.

Details in some anecdotes and stories have been changed to protect the identities of the persons involved.

Hardcover ISBN 978-1-60142-882-0
eBook ISBN 978-1-60142-883-7

Copyright © 2016 by Philip Wagner

Cover design by Kristopher K. Orr; cover image by Paul McGee, Getty Images

All rights reserved. No part of this book may be reproduced or transmitted in any form or by any means, electronic or mechanical, including photocopying and recording, or by any information storage and retrieval system, without permission in writing from the publisher.

Published in the United States by WaterBrook, an imprint of the Crown Publishing Group, a division of Penguin Random House LLC, New York.

WaterBrook® and its deer colophon are registered trademarks of Penguin Random House LLC.

Library of Congress Cataloging-in-Publication Data
Names: Wagner, Philip, 1953– author.
Title: Unlock your dream : discover the adventure you were created for / Philip Wagner.
Description: First edition. | New York : WaterBrook, an imprint of the Crown Publishing Group, a division of Penguin Random House LLC, [2016] | Includes bibliographical references.
Identifiers: LCCN 2016029471 (print) | LCCN 2016039683 (ebook) | ISBN 9781601428820 (hard cover) | ISBN 9781601428837 (eBook) | ISBN 9781601428837 (electronic)
Subjects: LCSH: Dreams—Religious aspects—Christianity. | Vocation—Christianity. | Self-actualization (Psychology)—Religious aspects—Christianity.
Classification: LCC BR115.D74 W34 2016 (print) | LCC BR115.D74 (ebook) | DDC 248.4—dc23
LC record available at https://lccn.loc.gov/2016029471

Printed in the United States of America
2016—First Edition

10 9 8 7 6 5 4 3 2 1

Special Sales
Most WaterBrook books are available at special quantity discounts when purchased in bulk by corporations, organizations, and special-interest groups. Custom imprinting or excerpting can also be done to fit special needs. For information, please e-mail specialmarketscms@penguinrandomhouse.com or call 1-800-603-7051.

**To all the dreamers . . .**

who imagine a higher version of your story.

**To all the dreamers . . .**

who have stumbled or have been knocked down along the way, who have been disqualified, dismissed, or overlooked, whose dreams are locked up somewhere in your soul but still have a flame of hope burning inside that causes you to imagine what could be.

**To all the dreamers who are fighters . . .**

to cancer survivors and to those who are still in the fight, to overcomers of the variety of life's battles, and to those whose dream is for those you love to keep fighting.

**To all the dreamers . . .**

who dare to believe, dare to trust, and are willing to take the risk, who start a business, express your art, sing your song, plant a church, create ideas, tell your stories, build a family, become humanitarians and philanthropists, loving people and changing the world, and who are willing to pursue the highest dream of your life—the God-dream.

**May you experience the elation of living the rest of your days in the joy of the dream.**

# Contents

# Interpreting Your Dreams

When I was a small boy in Kansas, a friend of mine and I went fishing, and as we sat there in the warmth of the summer afternoon on a river bank, we talked about what we wanted to do when we grew up. I told him that I wanted to be a real major league baseball player, a genuine professional like Honus Wagner. My friend said that he'd like to be President of the United States. Neither of us got our wish.

—President Dwight D. Eisenhower

My dream as a kid was to be the first white member of the Harlem Globetrotters, a basketball team made up of outstanding African American players. To me they were one of the best teams in the 1950s, '60s, and '70s. Back then, some of the great players, such as Wilt Chamberlain, played with the Trotters before joining the NBA. Not only were they an extraordinary basketball team; they were entertaining and earned the title Ambassadors of Goodwill, taking up humanitarian causes such as supporting campaigns with World Vision, inspiring at-risk youth, and entertaining US troops overseas.

Their basketball skills were second to none, and on top of that, they made people laugh. I loved how Meadowlark Lemon would always give his loud and humorous commentary on the game *while playing on the court,* and how they playfully harassed the referees and played tricks on the opposing team. Often they would bring a fan onto the court to be part of one of their pranks or would replace the game ball with a ball that had no air in it, or they would suddenly begin a game of "football" on the court. I loved them because they inspired me to think outside the box. As a kid, I imagined myself in their famous Magic Circle pregame routine, in which they set the tone for what was going to unfold in the game—dribbling between their legs, no-look passes, and unexpected trick plays. They had a perfect blend of superior skills and fun.

At home when no one was looking—well, even when someone was looking—I'd play my 45-rpm record of their theme song, "Sweet Georgia Brown," while I dribbled a basketball around the house. In my mind, I was on the court with the Trotters and I was so amazing, they didn't need Meadowlark or Curly Neal on the court.

Of course, you have probably already guessed that my childhood dream didn't come true. My aspirations of basketball fame are a distant memory. Like most children, I wished for something improbable.

A lot of first dreams are like that.

### Everyone Has a Dream

Many of us have those big dreams. We envision becoming rich and famous or winning the Powerball lottery. Some guys want to race in the Indianapolis 500 and win, while some girls dream of marrying Bradley Cooper. Although these dreams are fun to think about, the truth is that 99.9 percent of them will never be realized. (Sorry about that. Especially the Bradley Cooper thing.) My Globetrotter idea was one of those big, fanciful dreams that was great but didn't have a realistic shot of coming true. And like many childhood fantasies, it lasted only until another big-idea dream came into my mind. But that's the wonderful thing about these types of dreams—they have no boundaries. While most childhood dreams may be implausible, they teach us that dreams are wonderful goals to reach toward.

I live in Los Angeles, a place many people move to so they can pursue their big dreams. For more than thirty years, I've worked as a pastor at a church where many of those dreamers attend. A few years ago, I was walking down Hollywood Boulevard, known for the Hollywood Walk of Fame, where celebrities are given an actual star paying tribute to them and recognizing that they reached their dreams. As I watched people pass by, I wondered what their dreams were. Had their childhood fantasies been realized? Did their lives resemble anything close to those dreams, or had they taken on new aspirations?

As I maneuvered the street among the tourists, the locals, the young, the old, the rich, and the homeless, it occurred to me that Hollywood isn't the only place of dreams. No matter where I travel—New York, Nashville, or the rural areas of Africa—everyone I've encountered has a dream. So many people are inspired by them, some pursue them with passion, and others find that those aspirations are harder to reach than they'd expected. But we *all* dream. The capacity for dreaming and pursuing those dreams is a gift God has given each of us.

> *I think everybody should get rich and famous*
> *and do everything they ever dreamed of*
> *so they can see that it's not the answer.*
>
> —Jim Carrey, actor

Unfortunately, some people stop dreaming. They've tried and failed and grown frustrated. In their most difficult moments, whether wondering where the next meal will come from or becoming suddenly troubled by their own success, they whisper heartfelt words filled with familiar longing and heartache: "This isn't the life I dreamed of."

Every year people move to Hollywood by the thousands to pursue dreams that they believe will answer those longings. And thousands are crushed and heartbroken. A young woman I knew named Nicky was one. She moved to Los Angeles from Kansas to become a movie star. (Sounds cliché, doesn't it? . . . Kansas.) You might guess how the rest of this story goes. The girl came with high hopes and was met with frustration, loneliness, and discouragement. She discovered that this "following your dream" business is hard work. Okay, I'll just say it: it dawned on her that she was "not in Kansas anymore." She experienced rejections along the way, and the struggles she faced overpowered her desire to succeed. She learned the hard way that she needed to ask some important questions, the ones all of us ask at some time or another:

*Should my dream really take this much work?*

*Does trying this hard mean I'm on the wrong track?*

*Is the dream I'm following really the dream of my heart?*

*Should I quit and try something else, or should I be even more determined?*

*If I keep going the way I'm going, will I really find fulfillment?*

Those wonderings get to the heart of our deepest question: *Why am I really here?* When we begin to ask that question, we open ourselves to another kind of dream, one more significant and powerful.

## Another Kind of Dream

Some people follow their first dreams only to discover another kind of dream that involves reaching beyond themselves to change the world for others. Sometimes we go down one path, pursuing a vision of what we believe we are supposed to do, and then we discover we are meant to do something else. It may seem like a waste of time, but we likely would not have found the new path without taking the risk of pursuing that initial dream.

The path to these dreams of significance starts with that question: *Why am I here?* These dreams come from deep inside, and they inspire us to do and be better. They offer us significance, legacy, and a life well lived. They put our mark on the world and prove that what we do matters.

The power of these dreams is that every person is born to pursue them. *You* were born to pursue them. And best of all, unlike the childhood and big dreams we may harbor but not realize, these dreams absolutely can come true. I know because I'm living proof and I work with people every day who live out these dreams.

Jeff, a man in his thirties, is one of these people. He gathered up his wife and toddler and moved to Los Angeles to become a screenwriter. He thought, *If I don't try it now, I may never do it and I'll always wonder if I could have succeeded.* His dream was not so different from Nicky's, yet he *did* succeed. It didn't happen right away, but eventually doors opened and good things started to happen. Even though he struggled with the frustration and discouragement of each challenge or setback, he, unlike Nicky, became more determined. He knew he'd made the right decision. He was realizing his dream, and that kept him motivated. It wasn't his desire simply to become a famous and rich screenwriter; he felt compelled to write stories that would inspire people to live *their* lives with meaning, with a higher purpose, and to encourage them to fight to overcome their struggles. He wanted to use his gifts to influence others to be better people; he used his big dream to pursue a higher goal, which was his dream to achieve something of significance.

## A Higher Dream for You

As I continued my walk on Hollywood Boulevard, I could still smell the unique aroma of the previous night's trash in the alleyways by the restaurants. It blended with the smells of tourists with their coffees, croissants, and popcorn. The dichotomy of beauty and ashes that exists in a dream journey is vivid. I glanced down at the stars on the Hollywood Walk of Fame. Matt

Damon, Morgan Freeman, Billy Crystal, Kevin Costner, Katy Perry, Whitney Houston. Some stars represented those who had achieved great things in television, some for their work in movies, and some for music. Millions walk the sidewalk and wonder, *What would it be like to live this kind of dream?*

Suddenly I stopped. There at my feet was a star inscribed with Billy Graham's name. Yes, *that* Billy Graham, the evangelist who has preached live to 215 million people and additional millions through TV and radio.[1] I was struck by a realization. He was awarded that star for his achievements in television, but his dream wasn't to be a television celebrity. His dream of significance (*Why am I here?*) led him to do something with his life, which led him to an even greater goal.

I like to call it the God-dream. God-dreams are those special desires that come directly from God. They offer significance mixed with obedience to seek God's will and pursue what He wants to do in and through us. A God-dream is higher than any other dream.

> *I have a dream,* God whispers. *It's unfolding right now. It's larger than life. It is life itself. Lean closer. I will whisper this dream to your heart. It has been imprinted on your soul. You are part of My dream. You are My dream.*

Dreams are not unique to us! Our Creator God is a dreamer. He has vision and imagination, and He takes them and plants them in our souls. God gave you a specific desire, an assignment to complete, and it's something that will be larger than you and will fulfill you completely. He allows us to be part of His redeeming work, bringing a lost world back into communion with Him. God has a dream for our world, for humanity, and He has a dream for you and me. We have the capacity to reach those dreams, but it's crucial that our desires lead us to the God-dream for our lives.

The God-dream is better than we often think it will be. He always has more for us to achieve than we think we qualify for. Our greatest pursuit will be that dream.

For Billy Graham, his God-dream was for God to use him to preach the message of Christ's love to as many people as he could. It started with his simple obedience to follow God's purpose for him, and it grew beyond what Graham could ever possibly imagine. In 1949, Billy Graham scheduled a three-week series of revival meetings in Los Angeles. He called it the Greater Los Angeles Billy Graham Crusade at the "Canvas Cathedral with the Steeple of Light." News mogul William Randolph Hearst decided to give him national news coverage, some might say out of the blue. Hearst telegrammed his newspaper editors, telling them to focus on and promote Graham during the Los Angeles crusade. Five days later, Graham's local gathering had become a national phenomenon. Graham, then thirty years old, "drew 350,000 people over eight weeks to a huge tent revival at Washington Boulevard and Hill Street . . . five weeks longer than planned."[2]

Graham became an international figure not because he dreamed of fame and fortune but because he discovered God's dream for him—and God used him to touch the world.

You don't have to be a pastor to do something great. Preachers are not the only ones God calls or uses to influence the world for Christ. He uses everyone. That includes you. Think about that. He has special plans for you to accomplish. Those dreams you have in which you want your life to matter, to make a mark on the world, to be significant—God placed those dreams within you. He did it for a reason.

We are on this earth for a purpose. What we do and how we live matters, not just to us but to those on the receiving end of our realized dreams. And it matters to God.

The greatest discovery you can make is to learn what God has created you to accomplish. When you uncover your purpose, pursue it with diligence, and see the effects and power of that pursuit, you experience the adventure of a lifetime!

I know from experience that living out God-dreams is the best experience we can have. I didn't know what mine were all at once; my dreams became clearer and more focused as I went through different experiences. My big dreams and my significance dreams changed often in my first thirty years, but as I discovered my God-dreams and learned to trust them, I found that *all* my dreams became fulfilled. That's the beautiful part of God-dreams: the closer we move to God, the more our own dreams align with His. The fulfillment of my dreams went far beyond what I could have imagined or hoped for. My God-dream was to be a pastor, to help people by leading them toward Jesus. Today, the church I pastor, Oasis Church, is a diverse community for those who need healing and a refreshing encounter, for those who are wandering through life to find their way home, and for those who want to help others find their way. We reach world-changing leaders, celebrities, the weary, those who never had any interest in Jesus, and the down-and-out. Our church family includes young people, older people, millionaires, families living paycheck to paycheck, the influential, and the broken. Oasis is a place where God-dreams are fulfilled. Here, people find freedom and fun in the expression of their faith.

I thought that might be a big-enough dream, but God revealed even bigger dreams for me. I'm now a pastor of a thriving church; I travel all over the globe and speak on topics from having a passionate and genuine faith in Jesus Christ to leadership to reaching your God-dream to building healthy marriages and relationships. I've been married for more than thirty years, and I'm still in love with my wife. Miracles *do* happen. Love works. God-dreams are good dreams.

## The Allure of Lesser Dreams

Without intervention from heaven to understand why we are here and what our purpose is, we can entangle ourselves in lesser dreams. These are dreams that may make us feel good temporarily or might be impressive to others, but lesser dreams have little true impact on the world around us. Often they're more self-centered, dreams about *me* and improving *my* life. Or maybe they're the dreams we've settled for either because they are easier to reach or because we feel we've disqualified ourselves through some past failure.

Too often, when people go through life's battles, their dreams get locked away in their souls and are left there. These people never fully experience why they are here and what kind of power they can unleash when they dream the right kinds of dreams. They never learn how to unlock their God-dreams.

You may wonder, *Does it really matter if people don't discover and live out their dreams?* What's so wrong about living a "good enough" life, an ordinary life that doesn't necessarily change the world or make you famous but is livable?

Well, nothing. That is, if you're content to miss out on the great adventure God has planned for you. You have a dream. You long for something beyond the big-idea dreams, beyond the childhood fantasies, even beyond the good desires of marriage and family and career. You dream of significance, of reaching beyond yourself to pursue things that matter, things that last. And God has those dreams for you; in fact, His dreams for you are far better than the greatest dreams you can imagine. But we need to unlock them to actually reach them.

Attempting to reach your own dreams can be good practice for attaining the ultimate, the God-dreams for your life. The ones that God has for you are perfect. Plus the world needs you to reach them! They depend on you. They are cheering you on.

God has put something inside you. An image, an idea, or an assignment. Maybe you can't quite place it, but you know deep down it's there. If you take time to notice, you may discover that God is trying to get your attention. You just need to figure out what that dream really is, why you can't give up on it, and how you can unlock it to experience life at the greatest level. I'm going to help you do just that.

I want you to reach those dreams. I've met thousands of people who have moved to Los Angeles only to discover that the dream that brought them here isn't the dream they really want to live. I've met just as many people who have no idea what their dreams are. They know instinctively that dreams matter—I think we all do—but when asked to describe their dreams, they draw a blank.

I'm going to help you unlock your dreams so that God can do amazing things in and through you. Jesus reminded us that "with God all things are possible."[3] So nothing should hold us back!

Throughout this book, I'll share stories, my own and those of other dreamers, that can help you unlock dreams that have been shut down somewhere in your heart. Many times people get stuck in a season of life and can't seem to move forward toward the goal. Even though their dream is still important to them, they are not sure how to keep going. I'll identify some dream locks (things that keep us from pursuing our God-dreams), and I'll suggest some keys to unlock them (practical ideas that will help you go from where you are now to where you want to be—and where God wants you to be). I'll end each chapter with a scripture passage for you to read, reflect on, or even memorize so you can keep God's Word at the core of your heart and dreams.

I'm excited to begin this journey with you. I've been where you are, and I know the power of unlocking dreams in your life. The apostle Paul summed up well my prayer for you as you begin this path to unlocking your dreams:

We ask God to give you complete knowledge of his will and to give you spiritual wisdom and understanding. Then the way you live will always honor and please the Lord, and your lives will produce every kind of good fruit.[4]

Let's get started.

||| 

**DREAM LOCK:** Settling for lesser dreams or misinterpreting them may cause you to get stuck on a path that can jeopardize God's highest dream for your life.

**DREAM KEY:** Opening yourself to discovering and pursuing your God-dream will change your perspective and enhance your life pursuits. Look to God for His guidance, and allow Him to lead you not to the dreams you hoped for but to the dreams He *intends* for you.

**SCRIPTURE KEY:** Don't copy the behavior and customs of this world, but let God transform you into a new person by changing the way you think. Then you will learn to know God's will for you, which is good and pleasing and perfect. (Romans 12:2, NLT)

# Your Extraordinary, Ordinary Life

> I just try to live every day as if I've deliberately come
> back to this one day, to enjoy it, as if it was the full final
> day of my extraordinary, ordinary life.
>
> —TIM LAKE, IN THE MOVIE *About Time*

"What kind of work do you do?" The man sitting next to me on the plane had no idea why I paused before answering.

I usually hesitate when I hear this question. People have so many preconceived ideas about pastors. If I'm in the middle of an interesting conversation, I may not want the discussion to take a sudden awkward shift because I say, "I'm a pastor." It happens a lot.

I could give several different responses that would be accurate and stand a greater chance of keeping the conversation flowing. I could say any of the following: "I'm a writer." "I'm a speaker." "I'm the founder of a nonprofit organization, Generosity.org, that builds freshwater wells in developing nations." (That usually gets a great response.) Or to really keep the conversation lively, I could say, "I'm a retired assassin." Not that I have ever said that.

Don't get me wrong; I love my job. On most days. I have the honor of leading people into a personal and genuine faith. I get to make a positive difference in people's lives. When they find healing in their hearts from wounds of the past or find a joyful faith in Jesus, that's rewarding.

This day I simply and confidently declared, "I'm a pastor."

His hesitation was obvious as he processed this information. I knew he was thinking how to respond, and I began to consider if I should offer, "So how about those Dodgers?"

Finally, he said almost apologetically, "A pastor? Why didn't you say that earlier? I wouldn't have cussed so much."

"It didn't bother me."

And as I've experienced many times in the past, immediately the tone of the conversation changed. My reveal had put the kibosh on my hope for a genuine discussion. It became strained, surfacey, and he threw in a couple of religious references for good measure.

No one wants to be assigned a stereotype that is born in someone else's imagination, whether that image is created from the news, movies, or a bad experience the person may have had. Just like anyone else, I want the opportunity to define who I am.

My friend J John, who is an author and evangelist, tells of being on an airplane and talking to a lady who was a corporate CEO. She asked him, "What do you do?"

J John said, "Well, I work for a global enterprise. We've got outlets in nearly every country of the world! We run orphanages, we've got hospitals and hospices, and we feed the hungry and provide clothes for the poor. We do marriage and guidance counseling. We've got schools, colleges, universities, and publishing companies. We look after people from birth to death, and we deal in the area of behavioral alteration!"

"Wow!" she said.

"I know. It's amazing, isn't it?"

"What's it called?"

"It's called the 'church.' Have you heard of it?"

I love his description. He reminds me that I am part of something global, something amazing, and something that has a majestic significance beyond my own small imagination. His explanation reminds me that sometimes in my attitude, I default to a lower version of my work, my interests, or myself. I'm not the only one. People often describe themselves as "Oh, I'm just a manager of the sports department" or "I'm just a Starbucks barista" or "I'm just a mom." Just as I have at times, they've lost sight of the extraordinary part of who they are and what they do.

Too often we devalue our significance and lack the vision to see what God wants to do through us. That keeps us from discovering the extraordinary that permeates our ordinary lives. This holds us back from pursuing our dreams. Ordinary, everyday life really is quite extraordinary, and seeing this and experiencing it is exactly where we begin as we unlock our dreams.

## Recognizing the Extraordinary

J John's unique way of describing his job reminds me that I can sometimes forget the wonder of the work I've given my life to. I need to use something similar to his description more often. It's so easy to think I'm just an ordinary guy, doing an ordinary job. That kind of talk allows the relentless fog of mediocrity to impose its boundaries.

Secretly, we think that in order to pursue God-dreams of great significance, we have to *be somebody*. We look at others and compare ourselves with how much better they are. We think, *Of course we don't measure up to the extraordinary people around the world*—people like business mogul Bill Gates, humanitarian Mother Teresa, megachurch pastor Bill Hybels, innovator Steve Jobs, or entertainer Alicia Keys. There are, of course, many incredibly gifted people, but there are more ordinary people doing amazing things. We admire them. They inspire us. But it isn't only those gifted people; it can be the people around us. A mom who seems superhuman because her kids always behave, her life is organized, and she volunteers at the school and the homeless shelter. Or the businessman who is on every nonprofit board and constantly traveling somewhere to help the less fortunate.

Some people use their gifting, whether singing or leading, running a business or painting a work of art, and they make it look so easy that we think, *I wish I could do that.* We convince ourselves, *Those people are special. They are extraordinary. But not me.* Instead of embracing who God made us to be, we allow our insecurities to sabotage our thinking, which keeps our dreams locked away.

It causes us to compare our lives to others, and instead of looking to God for our significance, we look to others. I heard Steven Furtick, pastor of Elevation Church in Charlotte, North Carolina, explain, "The reason we struggle with insecurity is because we compare our behind-the-scenes with everyone else's highlight reel." We will always find ourselves lacking if we put our everyday normal stuff or our mundane-but-relentless life struggles up against the best days of someone else. We notice someone else's accomplishments on the days we feel like we may never reach our goals. We plug in to social media and see only the good things that others accomplish but don't see the hard times they go through to get there. We look on Instagram or Facebook and see our friends enjoying their vacations, but we don't see any posts about the work they did to earn those vacations. We look at our dreams and we think maybe ours aren't as important as someone else's. Insecurity can paralyze us from pursuing the very thing God has in mind for us.

If we allow them, those comparisons will establish a limiting perimeter in our minds until we have a moment of greater clarity, when we realize that every single one of those people—from Bill Gates to Alicia Keys—is just an ordinary person doing extraordinary stuff. And if *they* are ordinary, then we can be confident that *we,* who are also ordinary, can do extraordinary things too. That's when we have explosive potential. When we embrace the idea that God created us to be ordinarily extraordinary, we can envision dreams of significance; we can discover our God-dreams. And we can change the world.

How do we retrain our minds to focus on the extraordinary inside us rather than the insecurities that seem too real and overwhelming? A key is to focus on the reality that God can work through us to do more than we ever could do on our own.

We are not limited to our human weaknesses. We have been created in God's image,[1] and when we allow Jesus into our lives, His Holy Spirit comes alive inside us, giving us supernatural strength and power to pursue our God-dreams. God has put within us abilities that are greater than we realize. The apostle Paul said, "[God] is able to do immeasurably more than all we ask or imagine, according to his power that is at work within us."[2] We act like Clark Kent but have forgotten that we have some Superman going on inside us.

## Seeing Beyond "What Is"
## to Discover "What Could Be"

A couple of years ago I was unwillingly stuck in the nightmare rush-hour traffic that Los Angeles is famous for: the stop-and-go, parking-lot kind that can wear on your nerves in zero to sixty seconds. Everyone was tense.

When I approached a traffic light, I noticed that a car two vehicles in front of me had broken down. The light turned green and that car wasn't going anywhere—and neither was the rest of the line. Meanwhile, the person two cars behind me honked continually at the lack of movement.

I thought, *What am I going to do about this situation?* I got out of my car, and like a boss, I walked back to the man honking his horn. Through his rolled-up window, I said, "The lady's car is stalled in front of the line. I will sit here and honk the horn for you, if you will go help that woman fix her stalled engine."

The man looked at me with a face clearly marked with regret. "I'm sorry. You're right. I'm just frustrated."

Then I woke from my fantasy.

What I actually did was look at the guy through my rearview mirror and roll my eyes as I mumbled to myself, "Some people are jerks!" Then I pulled into the other lane and passed the stalled vehicle. I could have said something to that man, but then I remembered that some people carry guns in their cars. I could have helped the lady, but I don't know much about auto repair. So I let the moment pass without my intervention. What if, instead, that moment had led to something extraordinary? What if, by not doing something to help, I missed a key opportunity to do something that really mattered?

> *If you will do what others will not do, you can have what others will never have.*
>
> —Jerry Rice, athlete

I'm convinced that we miss many amazing moments because we don't see ourselves or our purposes as important. We forget that God is guiding us, and we neglect to seize those moments that could further our dreams.

Instead of embracing each day's ordinary moments and seeing the amazing work we can do through who we are right now, too many of us only look for those situations that seem extraordinary. We pass up ordinary opportunities to pursue our dreams because we're waiting for the "big" stuff to happen. Instead of seeing the value in spending time with someone who needs us, we pass up that opportunity to look for something that appears more glamorous or significant. We might secretly think that volunteering to lead a small group of five people isn't really pursuing our dream, so instead we sit around and do nothing while waiting for really big opportunities to appear that could allow us to impact hundreds of people.

We want to feel extraordinary several times during the day. But that perspective of life actually holds us back.

Did you see the movie *The Secret Life of Walter Mitty*, starring Ben Stiller? It was based on a 1939 James Thurber short story, which appeared in the *New Yorker*. Mitty was an ineffectual man who spent more time in heroic daydreams than paying attention to the real world. He imagined himself doing amazing things, like flying a navy airplane through a storm, performing a delicate and intense surgery, or sweeping a beautiful girl off her feet. He was so busy imagining greatness that he never quite accomplished anything of significance. He was trapped in his ordinary life, desperately wanting to be extraordinary.

The mistake Mitty made was that he spent so much time imagining about the extraordinary that he missed the truly extraordinary precious moments of life. He lacked the courage to take action.

While that is a fictional story, I've met plenty of people who live that way in real life. They talk about wanting to do great things of profound significance but miss the simplest opportunities to put those desires into practice. They fail to see what is directly in front of them.

The *extraordinary* you pursue may be hidden, but it is closer than you think. You will discover the extraordinary by opening your eyes to the opportunities around you and then taking action.

Jesus explained it this way: "Whoever can be trusted with very little can also be trusted with much."[3] We don't simply wake up one morning and discover how extraordinary we are, but as we do what we can, with what we have now, our extraordinary moments begin to evolve out of our actions.

Take a risk and dive into the everyday moments you encounter. You will discover brilliant surprises by being awakened to opportunities that arise "accidentally" as you go on your way. The day we realize that we have the capacity for a miraculous impact on others is the day that invites us on an ordinarily extraordinary journey to realizing our dreams.

Extraordinary moments are hidden in our ordinary days. Extraordinary abilities are locked inside our ordinary selves. But we have to look for them. We have to be present and in the moment. We can't let those opportunities and flashes of potential pass us by.

## Lessons Learned in a Strip Club

When I was eighteen years old, I wanted to pursue my desire to help people in desperate situations discover Jesus. So I went to work with a ministry on New Orleans's notorious Bourbon Street.

During the day I, along with several other young men and women, worked at the ministry office, and then after work we went out in teams and talked with strangers, sharing the hope that we'd found in Jesus. We'd offer to pray for them or provide help for more immediate needs, such as food or places to stay.

The experience definitely showed me how ordinary I was! Picture the most naive, clean-cut, inexperienced teenager you can think of. Yeah, that was me. I'm sure my eyes were in a constant state of wide-eyed shock and disbelief as I encountered people in all kinds of conditions: drunken, vomiting partiers; prostitutes (both male and female); unsuspecting college students looking for fun; successful businesspeople; and plenty more. But I wanted to reach out to them because I knew they needed Jesus. I was young and believed that God could do anything. I was dangerous and didn't know it.

Everywhere I looked my eyes met posters and billboards revealing sexy, partially clothed women, enticing people to stop in that club, have a few drinks, and watch the girls dance. Each night as I walked home after work, I noticed the picture of one particular girl. Among the hundreds of banners, her photo stood out to me. Not because she was sexy or beautiful, even though she was both, but something in her gaze showed an emptiness and pain, and I just couldn't shake it. Every day as I passed that billboard, walking to and from work, I prayed for that girl. I prayed that she would find Jesus, leave the sex industry, and find a higher way of living.

One night after we had finished our outreach, I headed back toward the YMCA, my home. When I walked by the club where the poster showed that the girl danced, I suddenly decided I needed to go in and let her know that Jesus loves her. I paced up and down the sidewalk for several minutes, my heart racing because I had no idea what to expect, but somehow I knew that it was something extraordinary. It was definitely a risk!

*Will I get thrown out? Am I about to do something extraordinarily stupid? Will they laugh at me? Will I look like an idiot when I have no idea what to say?* I could have answered those last two questions on my own! But I seized the moment. I walked in, and after they checked my ID to verify that I was actually older than the sixteen years I looked, I went over to the closest bar stool and sat. Unfortunately, it was against a dance platform positioned right behind the bartender.

"What do you want to drink?"

"Uh, do you have a 7Up or something?"

The bartender's eyebrows moved high on his forehead. "No alcohol?"

"No thanks. Just a 7Up," I tried to say with confidence. "I want to talk to the girl who's on the banner outside."

"You mean Hope? She'll be out in a minute. She's up next."

"Oh, well, I don't need to watch her . . . I mean . . . I just want to *talk* to her. Can she come out here before she dances?"

"What's this about?" His eyebrows now scrunched together in suspicion.

"I have something I've got to tell her."

He surveyed me for a moment, then with no emotion said, "I'll go tell her you're here."

My mind began to race. *What do I say when she comes out? This was a big mistake. What am I doing? I need to find the closest exit so I can scurry off to safety.*

I started mentally running through a list of all the reasons this was a bad idea. But most glaring, I kept thinking, *I'm not cut out for this assignment.* I could feel my heart diving into a dark downward spiral of self-doubt. *She'll think I'm some sort of jerk at best, a religious nut at worst.* My hands were clammy. My throat was as dry as a drought in the desert. I forced down another sip of 7Up. *I should have at least gotten a soda with caffeine,* I reprimanded myself.

*What a dork,* I thought. *I'm here to tell her about how* Jesus *can help her.* I glanced at my terrified pale self in the mirror of my mind. Judging between the two of us, *I* was the one who looked most desperate for help. I wondered if I had any business doing God's business.

The bartender returned. "She might come out here after she dances."

It's very hard to keep your focus on a glass of 7Up when someone is undressing—while holding a four-foot snake—and dancing ten feet from you. Yes. A snake. That part was a surprise. My already-overloaded senses were bombarded with the new and forbidden. I didn't know where to look—the 7Up, the bartender, the guy two stools over, or a quick glance at Hope. Wrong choice. Back to my 7Up.

*What's with the snake? Wait, there are two? Do people actually like watching someone dancing while holding a snake?*

When her performance ended she grabbed a robe—thankfully—and walked over to me.

She sized me up and down while chomping on a piece of gum. "They said you wanted to talk to me?" Her question seemed more like an accusation. She looked rough, and her makeup appeared to cover a hard edge to her face. Tough chick. Pretty, but tough.

My words leaked out with uncertainty. "Hi, my name is Philip. I work at this ministry that reaches out to people here on the street." I gave her a card. I thought using the phrase "on the street" sounded cool. I had no idea if anyone used that or not. "Have you heard of it?"

"No," she said as she chewed her gum and looked over the card.

"Well, I just came here to tell you that Jesus loves you."

"I'm Jewish."

This was going splendidly.

"He still loves you. He loves everybody." Was I grasping or was that a good response?

"I don't think I'm interested in this."

"Oh." I hadn't really thought out what I would say this far into the conversation. "I don't want anything from you. I just wanted you to know if you ever need someone to talk to or to pray for you, the office is about four blocks down." I pointed toward the right. "We're there for you." I sounded as if I were offering free legal advice.

"Okay. Well, thanks." If she had any interest, she didn't show it.

"I gotta get going. It was nice to see—I mean, meet—you." I stood, turned, and walked out quickly like someone who had just shoplifted something and hoped no one noticed.

On the walk home, I replayed the scene. *I did it. I can't believe I just did that. I'm never doing that again. That was incredible!* "How stupid was that?" I said out loud.

The next day, the fear had dissipated and a boldness emerged. When I got to the office, I couldn't wait to tell my coworkers about my adventure. We would often tell of people we had met on the street or prayed with, and even those who turned us down, so I told them my story.

The office pastor looked stunned. "You went inside? Philip, first of all, we always go in twos, never alone. You don't go out and share your faith by yourself in this neighborhood. Second, we *never* go inside a club or bar. We only talk to people outside." He sighed. "I know you meant well, but please don't ever do that again. We really work hard to protect the integrity of our ministry."

He was right. It seemed so obvious once he said it. I was embarrassed.

"I'm really sorry. I guess I got carried away." Then before I could stop myself, I blurted, "She danced with snakes. Do a lot of women on Bourbon Street dance with snakes?"

"She danced with *snakes*?" the pastor asked.

"Maybe we could pray for her anyway," I suggested. *After we pray for me and my stupid decisions.*

After our prayer, I went back to work in the shipping and receiving department and tried to keep that encounter out of my mind. I loved that I took a risk and survived, but I couldn't shake the remorse over disappointing the leaders.

A few hours into the workday the pastor walked into the shipping area. He wore a funny look. "Philip, someone is here to see you."

"See *me*?"

"I think it's the dancer you told us about," he said as a grin crept over his face. "Come on."

We went to see her in the reception area. On the floor at her side sat a small cage the size of a large purse.

When I glanced down, she replied, "They're my snakes."

The other workers subtly moved back toward the wall. She told us their names, but I can't remember for sure what they were. Maybe Diablo and Jezebel.

She appreciated that I had reached out to her. For the next couple of hours we talked about Jesus. We talked about His love, His acceptance, and His forgiveness. She struggled with the idea that faith in God, and Jesus specifically, could really make a difference in her life. Up to that point her view was that all religions were irrelevant to real life. As we continued to talk, it became clear that she was now considering the haunting reality that the "real life" she was living wasn't so real at all. #Emptiness.

We prayed for her, and she left. But she came back the next day, and we talked some more. She had more questions. She battled with the life she had lived and the life that she hoped she could live. Her burdens were slowly being exposed as she let us in on the unhappy relationships she suffered through. The reality of the love that Jesus was offering became more compelling than the versions of love she had experienced so far.

Then in a moment we were uncertain would ever happen, with tears in her eyes, she said, "I would like to pray and invite Jesus into my life." We prayed with her as we began to recognize the holy moment that had snuck up on all of us.

> *I have overlooked the true value*
> *of certain moments in my life until*
> *I reflected back on them as memories.*

Afterward we celebrated how we took someone's lesser dreams and helped her turn them into extraordinary God-sized dreams!

I learned a few lessons on that "mission" trip. First, when doing ministry out on the streets, go out to tell people about Jesus only with someone else who is strong in their faith. Second, men should not go into strip clubs to witness. Really! Third, and this one is seriously important, go ahead and do something extraordinary, even though it may feel extremely ordinary at the time. Obviously, my example was extreme and had flaws. But the beautiful part of it was that God took my willingness and used it to touch someone's life.

The evidence is overwhelming. I'm just an ordinary guy, but inside I have these dreams to do extraordinary things. The same is true of you. God put inside you dreams that offer opportunities to seize the ordinary moments and to turn them into something extraordinary.

God does not always call those who are qualified; He qualifies those He has called. And that was another important key to unlocking my dreams:

being willing. The apostle Paul reminds us that "if the willingness is there, the gift is acceptable according to what one has, not according to what one does not have."[4]

That means we don't have to be uncertain about our dreams, our abilities, our talents, or our ordinariness. We don't have to pursue what we think is greatness when true greatness, according to God's standards, is right in front of us every day, waiting for us to say yes.

I confess I have overlooked the true value of certain moments in my life until I reflected back on them as memories. But that day God used a naive, slightly crazy, stunningly ordinary kid who had extraordinary dreams. That kid said yes to the moment, and God used him to change the life of a woman living in the sex industry.

Imagine what He's waiting to do with extraordinary, ordinary you. Remember that God lives in you and strengthens you to do the incredible. Seize the moment. Say yes.

|||

**DREAM LOCK:** Becoming complacent or disengaged prevents you from seeing the extraordinary within the ordinary where God does most of His work.

**DREAM KEY:** God has put amazing abilities inside ordinary you! Don't allow the hopelessness that may arise when you think you are just ordinary to lock you out of your dreams.

**SCRIPTURE KEY:** Now to him who is able to do immeasurably more than all we ask or imagine, according to his power that is at work within us. (Ephesians 3:20)

# The Great Exchange

When one door closes, another opens; but we often look so long and so regretfully upon the closed door that we do not see the one which has opened for us.

—ALEXANDER GRAHAM BELL

When I was a kid, I used to watch the TV show *Let's Make a Deal*. The host, Monty Hall, would offer to exchange various items with the contestants, only they couldn't know what that exchanged item was until they decided either to trade or pass. The item might be in a gift-wrapped box on stage or hidden behind a curtain. Monty would say something like, "You just won this beautiful jewelry box. Now I will give you three hundred dollars for the jewelry box, or you can keep the jewelry box, because you never know what could be in one of those little drawers. *Or* you can pick what's behind curtain number one!"

People would cheer and yell out encouragement to the contestants. "Take the money!" "Take the curtain!" or "Keep the box!" even though there might be nothing in the drawers. Of course one of those drawers could also hold a diamond ring.

I usually wanted them to choose the curtain.

Sometimes the contestant would pick the curtain, and it would open to reveal an old broken bicycle. #Fail. The contestant, of course, would be disappointed by this downgrade. But sometimes, much to their great excitement, waiting behind the curtain would be a brand-new car or a vacation to

Paris. The pressure of choosing between what the contestants had in their hands and the possibility of something better was the tension in the show and what made it so thrilling.

Sometimes we have an idea about our dreams but later discover something even better is waiting for us. When we let go of what we think is good in order to open ourselves to something better, we make what I call the great exchange. This exchange, letting go of what we know for what we don't know, can be scary when we have held on to one idea for so long.

Our exchange may involve changing the career we thought we wanted for one that is actually more rewarding and meaningful. The exchange could be related to a shift in our priorities over time. The trade is always about accepting a higher version of our dream because God sees us with greater capacity than we do. It's like trading our black-and-white, two-dimensional dream for God's full-color, 3-D, high-definition version. We might need to exchange the limited version of a dream that is steeped in self-achievement alone and make the life-altering shift to embrace a dream focused on making a difference in the world around us.

> God never asks us to give up something
> that is greater than His dream for us.

Ultimately, the exchange is all about trust. *Can I trust God with this dream I've been holding? Can I trust that, if I give up what I now have or what I'm pursuing for what God has for me, I will be trading up?* Our emotions, expectations, and even outside influences scream conflicting opinions, like the *Let's Make a Deal* audience, about what we should do. We have to decide, *Can I trust that God knows what's best?* God never asks us to give up something that is greater than His dream for us.

When it comes to deciding whether to keep what you have or trust God with what He has "behind the curtain," God's plan is always an upgrade. In Romans 12:2, Paul reminds us that the will of God for us is perfect. If we accept His dream and direction for our lives, it will be good and acceptable to us. Trust is not a euphemism for something else. Trust is the key. Take what's behind the curtain!

## Why Isn't My Dream Good Enough?

As we realize what really matters in life, we discover that many of our dreams need renovation, editing, and refinement. While we might aspire to something good and worthy, it may not be how God wants us to use the gifts He has given us.

Dreams that were right and God centered for one season of our lives may not remain so for all of our lives. God wants us to grow, evolve, and constantly reach for His highest. In other words, the dream He gave you for your early twenties may change once you have learned or accomplished what He wanted for that phase. No one but God knows how our life stories will exactly play out. It's a great thing to make plans, but along the way we have to adjust to the unexpected changes life throws at us. New ideas and desires emerge as we grow though different seasons. We have to recognize that our God-dream will become more evident and easier to interpret if we are willing to make the exchange. Just as our childhood dreams of being the first astronaut to go to Mars may need to be reevaluated as we grow up, so do our dreams for significance. With each course correction, if we are following Him, we exchange "up."

Our God-dream is not just about the destination or achievement alone; it's about what we discover and who we become along the way. When something comes up that seems to directly oppose the dream as we understand it, sometimes this makes us question whether our dream is right, if it's really from God, or if it's just our own idea. Praying for clarity about God's will for our dreams and searching in His Word, we eventually find a place of confident trust.

I find this place of confidence by allowing myself enough time to interpret what God's higher plan may be and by allowing God to reveal more to me. I don't think anything in my life has turned out 100 percent the way I thought it would. It isn't always easy, but if we can trust God, more clarity will emerge.

## How Do I Know What I Need to Exchange?

Figuring out the difference between our dream and the God-dream is a huge part of the process. This transition may include a lot of unknowns. People who successfully reach their dreams usually have to unravel some clues for discerning if they are aligned with God. We need to ask more than "What is my dream?" because that only gives us part of the answer.

If we are reluctant to pursue a God-dream and cling instead to our own creations, we will ultimately be dissatisfied. Lesser dreams never fulfill us completely. They never work out as well or are as glamorous as we had initially envisioned.

> *Our God-dream is not just about the destination or achievement alone; it's about what we discover and who we become along the way.*

If I'm unsure at some point, one eye-opening question I always ask is, "What are some needs around me right now that I can do something about?" The needs might seem unrelated, but I've always found that God shows me more of what I need to know when I'm available to help people.

I often write my thoughts and prayers in a notebook. It's like a journal, but it also is a kind of dream notebook. I write a few questions in my note-book about my ideas and desires so I can untangle them from any personal bias that may confuse my direction.

*Does this idea distract me from God's plan, or are they somehow connected?*

*Is there something I need to develop in myself that will help prepare me?*

*Is my dream what I thought it would be when I was younger? In what ways has it changed?*

*How should I approach reaching the dream as I understand it right now? What are the next steps?*

By asking questions like these for any dream or idea I want to pursue, I can filter out distractions to be sure I am moving toward God's dream. Though other dreams can be meaningful, we can't allow them to take the place of God's main dream. The Bible tells us how Satan once tried to im-plant his own dream in place of the God-dream in Jesus's life:

> The devil led [Jesus] up to a high place and showed him in an instant all the kingdoms of the world. And he said to him, "I will give you all their authority and splendor; it has been given to me, and I can give it to anyone I want to. If you worship me, it will all be yours."
>
> Jesus answered, "It is written: 'Worship the Lord your God and serve him only.' "[1]

When honoring God is our priority, it will lead us to God's plan and His assignment.

## When We Mistake Our Dreams for God's

One of the most fascinating stories in the Bible is the story of Joseph. Joseph was one of twelve brothers in a dynamically dysfunctional family. Favorit-ism, jealousy, hatred, attempted murder, and lies colored their world. He was

Jacob's son—as in "Abraham, Isaac, and Jacob"—so he had an important lineage.

God gave Joseph a dream. Literally.

One night Joseph had a dream, and when he told his brothers about it, they hated him more than ever. "Listen to this dream," he said. "We were out in the field, tying up bundles of grain. Suddenly my bundle stood up, and your bundles all gathered around and bowed low before mine!"

His brothers responded, "So you think you will be our king, do you? Do you actually think you will reign over us?" And they hated him all the more because of his dreams and the way he talked about them.[2]

Joseph thought this dream meant he was more significant than his brothers. He *thought* he understood his God-dream, but his understanding was shallow and self-centered. "Hey, guys, listen to this. I had a dream. It was clearly a God-dream. It was so cool. *I'm* gonna be important. *I'm* gonna be significant. And basically, y'all are gonna end up bowing down to me. You'll be like, 'Where would we be without Joseph?'"

This didn't go over well. It led to betrayal, deception, and a seventeen-year journey of enslavement and imprisonment.

To be fair, it's not unusual to interpret our dreams in a way that makes us look important. (*I want to make a difference in the world, not stay in this small town working at this fast-food place. I want to really do something with my life.*) It could be that Joseph needed to feel important. His brothers hated hearing about this dream in which he was going to be lifted up and be cooler than they were. It's pretty hard to take it when Joseph implies, "I'm going to be famous, and you all will be glad that you know me."

Sometimes our dreams are so exciting, we forget that humility is an essential part of making them successful. Unfortunately, at this stage, Joseph didn't possess that trait.

Joseph needed to untangle his understanding of the dream (his version) from God's. And that took time, maturity, and some hard lessons along the way. It took more than twenty years to see what God's dream for him was really about. God's version was very different from what he first imagined.

In our search for significance and our desire to impact the world, we might pursue a dream that feels like a God-dream, but our motivations can interfere with what God wants us to accomplish. If accepting God's plan makes us afraid that we are going to lose prestige, we might struggle in accepting it.

God-dreams are the highest form of dreams we can have. But unlocking them includes clarifying what they really are. To do this we need to untangle our understanding of God's plan from our own initial interpretation of our dreams.

Life can get distorted and our dream pursuit can become complicated. Left to our own imagination, without God's guidance, we can entangle ourselves in lesser dreams. Those are dreams where *we* are the focus, the star, the center of our universe. If we are going to put everything we have into our dreams, we need to be sure we understand what that dream is really about and that it *is* actually what God wants for us. How exactly can we untangle our dreams from God-dreams? Joseph's story can help us with that.

## Exchanging Our Expectations for Reality

We need to weigh our expectations against reality. Joseph had a great dream, but he needed help to interpret it accurately. I mean, he needed a lot of help. Misinterpreting God's dream can lead to expectations that frustrate us and to disappointment that can negatively affect our decision-making. Is the call really to be a dominant power figure? Or could it be the role of a servant?

As a side note, I'm a little leery of dreams people have while they are asleep. God does give people dreams at night because we read that in Scripture. But I've heard about so many strange dreams that it's hard to tell if they were from God or because the dreamers ate spicy Indian food before they went to bed. #I'mJustSayin'.

Dreams can be misleading. We can have crazy, weird, or unreasonable ideas that are firmly lodged in fantasyland. We need to get out of that place in order to reach the land God's dream is leading us to.

Joseph had to exchange his expectations about the dream for its reality. He expected his brothers to bow down and be grateful to have him in their lives. That wasn't the dream God had in mind, however. When Joseph's brothers threw him down a well and then sold him into slavery, Joseph's reality came quickly crashing in.

Unrealistic expectations bring frustration, but realistic expectations bring clarity. This kind of clarity usually takes time and maturity.

For a long time I wanted to write songs and be in music ministry. When I was in my late teens and early twenties, I realized I was going to be in ministry. I love music, and in the 1970s, contemporary Christian and worship music were becoming popular. So I decided that God wanted me to be a Christian artist. I began singing at churches and youth gatherings. I recorded two albums with a sub-label of Maranatha! Music, although they didn't sell many copies.

I once sang at a prison chapel, and just before I went on stage, the chaplain said, "They love hearing music, especially if there is a band or pretty girls who sing with you." I was singing by myself with an acoustic guitar. By the third song, I had cleared the room from seventy hopeful prisoners to about eight who remained captive in the service. Some of them were clearly too uncomfortable to leave with the others, even though they probably wanted to. (I can now scratch "Clearing a room of dangerous prisoners" off my bucket list.)

I loved music, and while I may have reached some people through my songs, this dream was driven mostly by my own desires. When I got honest with myself, I realized that while I might be good with music, I was far from great, and God had given me talents in other areas that I could use more with more impact. After a few years of trial and error, I had to exchange expectations for reality and accept that the singing ministry was my idea, not God's. I think God just gave me my music gifts because He wanted me to sing for my own enjoyment . . . and maybe His.

But how do you know what's realistic and what isn't? These three keys will help you stay focused as you untangle your expectations from reality.

### Key 1: It May Take Longer Than You Think

Let me say right away that this is not my favorite key. Joseph discovered through his experience that it takes time for the dream to come together—decades in his case. Don't panic! I'm not suggesting that your dream will take twenty or thirty years. Joseph took that initial dream and piled his expectations on it, and that can cause more delays than a traffic jam on the freeway. Then his brothers ganged up on him and sold him as a slave. Detour.

He was carried off to Egypt and Potiphar purchased him. Joseph did well then, but then Potiphar's wife wanted a little more service than Joseph was comfortable giving, and he ended up in prison under a false charge of attempted rape. More detours?

It's interesting that Joseph, who started out not being the best at interpreting his own dream, gained a reputation in prison as a reliable interpreter of other people's dreams. One man's dream revealed that he was going to get a pardon, a "get out of jail free" card. Joseph told the man to remember him after his release. Since the man was going to work for Pharaoh, Joseph asked him to put in a good word for him. The man agreed—and then promptly forgot for two years. Two. Years. (Important side note: sometimes people forget to give you the same support you've given them.) Fortunately, Joseph had matured some, so he didn't get wigged out because the man failed to follow through on Joseph's release plan. But two years later, God caused the man to remember, and when Pharaoh had a dream that his usual interpreters could not explain, guess who he called to help him figure it out?

Joseph listened to the dream and explained that seven years of plenty would be followed by seven years of famine. As a reward Pharaoh placed Joseph in a key position in the kingdom. You see where this is going, right?

God used Joseph's dream-interpretation skill, which had initially gotten Joseph into trouble, to bring about his promotion. Sometimes God wants us to wait because of timing, and sometimes God wants us to wait because He needs to develop us into people able to accomplish His purpose. That was Joseph's dream exchange: he had to exchange his interpretation for trusting that God had the right one.

Through all those years of waiting, had God forgotten about the dream He gave Joseph? (If you're keeping score at home, the answer is no.) Did Joseph forget about it or lose hope? No, he trusted and stayed faithful. What Joseph didn't see was that each time, God was still at work behind the scenes to bring about another major step in His plan.

When we allow Him, God is really good at getting us where He wants us to be. He strategically positions us in the right place at the right time. The challenge is, the right place often seems like the wrong place, and the right time often seems like the wrong time.

Sometimes the reality is that we have an idea of the dream we want to pursue, but we can see only one piece of the plan at a time. I've coached people in their twenties who expect to get the whole plan before they start moving forward. It's unrealistic to expect to know every detail from the beginning. It's more likely that you will have the same journey most of us have had, which is to reach our dreams by heading out in the right direction without having the entire road map laid out.

Don't become immobilized because you don't know the whole plan right now. Don't be afraid of that place between living in your current circumstances and reaching your dreams. That time is never static or wasted. Do what you know to do now, and keep moving forward. Even when you don't see where the plan is headed, or when it feels like a dead end, you can be assured that God is still working.

### Key 2: There Is a Greater Cost Than You May Realize

Joseph took a big risk by interpreting Pharaoh's dream. If Pharaoh didn't like what Joseph said, he could have had him executed. Joseph had to trust the gift that God had given him. He had to trust the message God was giving him to deliver to Pharaoh. The greatest cost was the years Joseph spent trusting God, being faithful with what God put in front of him, and allowing a new Joseph to emerge.

More than two decades had passed since his brothers had sold Joseph into slavery and deceived their father, Jacob. Then the famine brought the brothers to him. And there they were, bowing down to Pharaoh's second in command: Joseph. They looked a lot like the eleven bundles of wheat seen in a dream years ago, only Joseph wasn't gloating now. He realized that God had brought him to this moment for His purposes. Now Joseph wanted to do things right.

We can't always tell that God is using the current situation to get us ready for the next phase. Following God today leads us to where we need to be tomorrow. Having to attempt something beyond our perceived capabilities does not mean the dream is unreasonable, but it is the trade-off for accomplishing big things. Through the act of preparing for something amazing, amazing begins to happen inside us. But it may come at a cost.

Looking at things strictly from a human point of view, Joseph lost decades of his life. He lost his family; essentially he was stripped of everything dear to him so that God's purposes could occur. Obviously not all dreams will include that level of sacrifice, but perhaps we need to expect that dreams that have true, eternal significance *will* cost us something. Jesus reminds us that we need to be willing to step away from our families and everything we love in order to follow Him: "You cannot be my disciple, unless you love me more than you love your father and mother, your wife and children, and your brothers and sisters. You cannot come with me unless you love me more than you love your own life."[3]

God-dreams will always cost us something, but the rewards are greater gains than we can ever imagine.

### Key 3: It Takes Work to Reach a Worthy Dream

Joseph didn't have a dream and then just go out and step into that reality. It's not even that he had to study hard to earn a degree to lead him to his dream. He was a slave! He did hard labor for years before he got where God was leading him.

It took more work for Joseph, and it usually takes more work for us than we think it will. It is a fantasy to believe that our dreams will just unfold. John Grisham is a great example. He was an attorney and a state legislator but always wanted to be a writer. His career kept him busy, but with the dream of writing a novel, he got up early each day to write one page. Within a few years, he had written *A Time to Kill*. But it wasn't a success right away. No editor would look at it, and his manuscript was rejected by twenty-eight publishers. Finally Wynwood Press, an unknown publisher, agreed to a modest five-thousand-copy print run. He didn't become an overnight sensation. It came with years of work. Today, he has sold more than three hundred million books, but it all started by not being too lazy to write just one page a day.[4]

I've found that those who are the most fulfilled are those who are willing to pay the price to make their dreams come true. Your dream will take work, so don't shy away from doing what you need to do to keep moving ahead.

## Exchanging Requires Attitude Adjustments

Along the way we will need to make attitude adjustments. Joseph faced a lot of obstacles—being sold into slavery and suffering betrayal by his boss's wife, among others—and he had to work on the attitude of his heart over each of these experiences. Joseph wasn't ready to handle what God had planned for him—and for all of Egypt. God needed to prepare him.

The writer in Psalms tells us, "Until the time came to fulfill his dreams, the LORD tested Joseph's character. Then Pharaoh sent for him and set him free; the ruler of the nation opened his prison door."[5]

Whatever dream God has planned for you, it's big enough that you need some time to prepare. That means God may need to adjust your attitude. Often it's when life goes sideways that we discover how to handle people and situations with grace. On the road to reaching our dreams, when we stumble or face obstacles, those are the times we learn about the places in our hearts that need to be renovated. We learn perseverance, the quality that allows all other qualities the time to develop. I've had to learn, among other things, that the *goal* is more important than the *role*. Why is it that the title I have or the bio I use becomes so important to me that I lose sight of what my purpose was all about in the first place?

As we surrender our will and attitude to God, He develops our character. Usually the worst thing that can happen is for us to reach our dream before our character can handle it. That was certainly true for Joseph. I'm talking about the character required to be honest, genuine, and true to our values. Without this kind of integrity, our values are not what we present them to be. They are just good ideas. This inconsistency can be devastating to our dreams.

The next time you face an obstacle on the path to fulfilling your dream, surrender it to Christ and allow Him to adjust your attitude.

## Exchanging Involves Course Corrections

Along the way we'll need to make some course corrections. Joseph had to exchange his approach to the dream and trust God's plan. That meant God's timing and God's way. Joseph thought he was ready to become a great leader and that his dream was a sign that God was ready to roll right then. Instead he spent years going through tough trials and disappointments. During times like this it's easy to question God's plan.

Understanding *what* the dream is will be crucial, but *how* we approach reaching that dream and *when* to do it is just as important.

I always felt like I was ready for my next *promotion* in life, but often my plans were formed without knowing valuable information. We probably will always think we are ready to start before God knows it's time. If we aren't careful, we'll start trying to help God out and get ahead of Him. That's when we start implementing stupid plans.

It is human nature to want to see our dreams fulfilled *right now*, but God's timing is the best. Would we allow our ten-year-old to drive a car? We want our child to learn to drive someday but probably not this day.

## Our Dreams Affect Other People

Joseph had to realize that his dream had less to do with personal importance and more to do with how he was going to help others. That meant he had to honor others along the way. Joseph's first mistake was telling his family about his dream and how it meant they would bow down to him. His behavior dishonored his brothers and his father. It also dishonored God and the position God intended for him. Joseph learned a hard lesson about honor, which was particularly important when he was sold into slavery and had to honor authority.

As he learned to honor others, the Lord allowed him to prosper in the house of his Egyptian master. Potiphar put him in charge of his household, and he entrusted to his care everything he owned. God also blessed everything Potiphar had, both in the house and in the field, all because Joseph submitted to God and allowed Him to adjust his expectations and attitudes. Because of that, God also blessed the people around Joseph.[6] That's an amazing gift and a sobering responsibility.

I wish I could say that I have always pursued my God-dreams in ways that were wise and honored those around me. But at times, especially early in my ministry, I have been careless with people I worked with. I had to increase my abilities as a leader. I've had to change my attitude. I've needed to make things right with those whom I've hurt, so I've gone back many times and apologized. This is part of the pursuit of our dreams. What we do and how we do it always has a ripple effect on others.

## Focus on Maturing as a Person

For our dreams to flourish, we have to invest time in our character growth. Joseph had to exchange who he thought he was for the man God needed him to be. When he finally saw his dream unfold, he was a different person. He had become a man who could be trusted to serve God's purpose. It was no longer about Joseph's ego; it was about God's plan.

God decides the sphere of our influence. He decides the scope of our impact. We decide if we will be faithful with what is right in front of us. We make mistakes when we assume or try to determine things for ourselves instead of trusting God to lead us. Proverbs 16:9 tells us, "In their hearts humans plan their course, but the LORD establishes their steps."

My dream was to be a pastor. I imagined preaching to thousands of people. Overnight. But I learned that the outcome is not in my control. What is in my control is to preach to one hundred people—or ten, or *one*—with the same dedication that I would if it *were* a thousand. Jesus reminds us that when we are faithful in handling small tasks, He will give us many more responsibilities.[7]

And that comes when we exchange our wants and ideas of what our dreams should be with what God wants for us. When we give up control of our expectations, we discover that God's dreams for us really are higher and greater than our limited understanding.

I've learned to pray, *Show me your ways, Lord, teach me your paths. Guide me in your truth and teach me, for you are God my Savior, and my hope is in you all day long.*[8] That keeps me focused on God's purposes rather than getting carried away with my own.

Don't allow your impatience or your insistence that you can do it on your own keep you from what God has planned. Trust where He is leading you, and pay attention to everything and everyone He puts on your path. All of it is shaping and preparing you to realize your God-dream.

|||

**DREAM LOCKS:** Expectations for how your dreams should look can keep you stalled for years.

**DREAM KEY:** No dream God gives you is insignificant. Each of your steps and pursuits serve to move you toward the big dream He has intended for you.

**SCRIPTURE KEY:** Patient endurance is what you need now, so that you will continue to do God's will. Then you will receive all that he has promised. (Hebrews 10:36, NLT)

# Distractions, Divine Interruptions, and Defining Moments

All men dream: but not equally. Those who dream by night in the dusty recesses of their minds wake in the day to find that it was vanity: but the dreamers of the day are dangerous men, for they may act their dream with open eyes, to make it possible.

—T. E. LAWRENCE, *Seven Pillars of Wisdom*

Sometimes my life is so filled with distractions, I find it difficult to figure out exactly what I should be paying attention to. I start cooking something in the kitchen and see something that belongs in my office. So I go to the office to put it away, sit to check my e-mail, go on Facebook instead, decide to write a note, and twenty minutes later I realize that what I was cooking has burned. I realize this because the smoke detector is reminding me that I forgot something.

Most people can relate to these types of distractions. I have ADD, so *anything* can distract me! Often my family or friends say, "Earth to Philip." It seems like our entire society has a type of ADD. It's rare to have a conversation with someone who doesn't look at his or her cell phone to check a message or a notice. There are many options of what can take our focus away in our technology-driven world.

By the way, if you wonder whether you have your own personal ADD or society's version, you probably have ADD if (1) you are driving down the street and notice you have the TV remote in your hand, (2) you buy a shirt at the store and go home to realize that you bought that same shirt four weeks ago and forgot about it in your closet, or (3) you get distracted by this side note and forget you were reading an amazing book.

A few years ago I took nine-year-old Shemar, from our church, with me to a Dodgers baseball game. Apparently the game wasn't interesting enough for him, so when the fans began to do the wave and it reached our section, Shemar jumped to his feet with great joy. I didn't join in.

"I'm philosophically opposed to people doing the wave," I explained. "My reasoning is simple: just because *you* are bored doesn't mean there isn't something really important going on." I glanced at my companion, looking for a nod of acknowledgment to show he understood this profound insight.

That nod never came.

Regardless, I pushed on. "Every player out there always has a strategy in mind or a play on the field he is considering. Just because people don't understand what is going on out on the field, that doesn't mean they should distract everyone else."

Shemar followed the crowd as the wave of raised arms headed back around.

"If this batter gets on base, he will represent the tying run."

"This time you should stand up too!" he suggested with enthusiasm. My mentoring moment did not distract him from what brought him so much joy. The wave.

It wasn't that I didn't want to have fun. I just wanted to focus on the *actual game*.

Focus really *is* important as we pursue our dreams. I can get so distracted by chasing the big-picture stuff that I miss the smaller, more significant issues that are just as important. I've missed so many great moments because I've been distracted by what I thought I could or should be doing. Does this happen to you? One distraction leads to another, which leads to another, and before we know it, we're off course and we wonder how we'll ever reach our dreams.

> *Distractions might actually be heavenly interruptions designed to lead us into an important new piece of the puzzle for God's ultimate plan for our dream.*

One big distraction that can derail our dreams is financial concerns. Have you ever thought something like this?

*If I didn't have to work, I'd pursue my art.*

*If I didn't have so much debt, I'd start my own business.*

*If I had more money, I'd travel the world and do mission work.*

Obviously we don't want to make foolish choices that can make life harder, and it won't make sense to pursue every dream, but sometimes we allow money worries to keep us from seeing the possibilities.

Maybe we regroup and decide to stay focused on the main thing and not allow anything to disrupt us. Only that doesn't work either because those distractions might actually be heavenly interruptions designed to lead us into an important new piece of the puzzle for God's ultimate plan for our dream. What if we stay so busy pursuing what we think we're supposed to do that we miss the very things right in front of us that *are* part of unlocking our dream?

The apostle Paul tells us, "Be very careful, then, how you live—not as unwise but as wise, making the most of every opportunity."[1] The real challenge is, how do we know what is a distraction and what is an opportunity?

## Distractions or Divine Interruptions?

One day I had just gotten my favorite coffee drink from Starbucks and was walking down Wilshire Boulevard near our church. I was thinking about some of the important stuff that often fills my mind, like how to reach more people in Los Angeles for Jesus and what the New York Yankees should do about their current hitting slump. As I walked past a newspaper machine, a headline caught my attention: "Estimated 1.1 Billion People Don't Have Access to Clean Water."

*That can't be right,* I thought. *No, that has to be wrong. I'm going to research this when I get home.*

So I did. I put all my other have-tos on the back burner, sat at my computer, and began to research this claim. What I discovered stunned me. The information was correct: 1.1 billion people.[2] About one out of every six people on the planet doesn't have clean water.

*Is this common knowledge and I'm just figuring this out?* I wondered.

I couldn't get this new information out of my mind. I was reflecting on it when I unconsciously dumped a half-full glass of water down the drain because I didn't want to finish it. I realized, *I just pour out water like there's an endless supply! A billion people are trying to save the drops like they are gold.*

I started talking to people about it. "Did you know that 1.1 billion people don't have clean water to drink or cook with?"

The responses were similar: "Are you kidding me?" "Are you sure?" "I didn't know that."

That number was so massive it was difficult to wrap my brain around it: one *billion* people. I decided I had to do something about it! I might not be able to help millions of people, but I could help some of them.

One day while I was in the grocery store buying salad dressing, I noticed the Newman's Own product line. Actor Paul Newman used his influence to create a company whose profits go to charity. I thought again about the water crisis and how I might be able to create something we could sell to raise funds for this need.

*I don't have that kind of influence,* I reasoned, *but I do have some. I can use what I do have to help these people.*

As a pastor I could let people in our church community know about this global problem and raise money for the cause. Taking our cue from Paul Newman, we purchased bottles of water in bulk. We printed labels that read *Generosity Water,* and then we gave them to people in our church for a donation, which would help fund wells. By including information about the global water crisis on each bottle, we educated people and communicated the idea that while they are buying water, they are also giving water to others, thus the name: Generosity Water. My dream to help others in crisis grew.

The people in our church got on board right away with my dream, and we partnered with organizations, such as World Vision and others, that were already involved in this work. I invited Scott Harrison, the founder of charity: water, to speak to our church and tell us more about the water crisis. He inspired us, and we financed several wells with his organization. We funded a big water system for Watoto Child Care Ministries in Gulu, Uganda, which stores and purifies water for their children's homes. We also built a ten-toilet latrine for a school in Peche Village near Gulu.

The more we helped, the more we learned about the related issues. We discovered that the water crisis creates huge obstacles to improving education in the developing world. Fetching water often falls on women and children, preventing them from working or getting an education. On average, they spend four hours each day collecting water. And when a child's day is spent fetching clean water or battling a water-related disease, attending school is simply not possible. Providing access to clean water relieves this burden and unleashes the freedom to work, learn, grow, and dream. Access to clean water helps women get the same opportunities as men to help provide for their families.[3]

We discovered that "the lack of clean water and sanitation causes 80% of all sickness and disease in the developing world—affecting more people than war, AIDS, and famine combined. . . . Teaching people to wash their hands and properly use latrines saves more lives than any vaccine. In fact, sanitation and hygiene programs double the impact of every water project—decreasing disease in a community by an average of 47%."[4]

With each new discovery about the water crisis, we became more committed to doing something about it. Over the past eight years, we have drilled wells near schools, churches, and town squares. We have built latrines, donated school supplies, and made available sanitary pads for the girls going to school.

As the years have gone by, the dream continues to expand. In 2008, I asked my son, Jordan, to take leadership, and he created the nonprofit foundation now named Generosity.org.[5] Through his direction, the organization has taken huge leaps forward. By 2016 we had funded more than seven hundred wells for water projects in nineteen nations.

More than four hundred thousand people have access to clean water because my attention and focus were interrupted that day when I noticed the newspaper headline and decided to do some research and follow God's lead.

> *What feels like an interruption in one moment can be the key to unlock another direction from God.*

What feels like an interruption in one moment can be the key to unlock another direction from God. But how do you tell the difference between a distraction and a divine interruption? There is no "one size fits all" checklist to evaluate this. One way to figure it out is to determine whether your current path honors God's true direction or whether the new direction you are being drawn to may be more aligned with His purpose for you.

I know that on our way He will lead us to do a few projects that may be short-term assignments that do not interfere with His ultimate direction. I don't believe God will distract you, however, from what He wants you to do with something that doesn't ultimately add to His purpose or benefit His people. I always try to discover this through praying and carefully reading and reflecting on God's Word.

Another way to help assess this is to be patient and allow God to reveal more clearly to you what direction to take. Time is your friend. When you react to a situation too quickly and do not give it thoughtful consideration, it's easy to be misled into thinking a distraction is a divine interruption and vice versa.

I rely a lot on input from spiritual leaders and people I know who model making wise decisions. I watch how they handle distractions and opportunities. I talk to them about my situation and ask for their advice and guidance.

King Solomon said, "Plans fail for lack of counsel, but with many advisers they succeed."[6] This habit of looking to other strong leaders has helped me so many times.

Jesus is a great role model for us to consider. He was always available for interruptions. He kept Himself open so He could turn what looked like a distraction into a gateway to a miracle.

There was the day when Jesus was teaching and some parents took their children to Him so He would pray over them and bless them. The disciples scolded the parents for bothering Jesus; they saw the children as a disruption. But Jesus said, "Let the little children come to me, and do not hinder them, for the kingdom of heaven belongs to such as these."[7] He recognized the opportunity to teach His followers about the kind of faith they needed. How did He know the difference between distraction and divine interruption? Because He stayed close to the Father, listening for and following God's leading.

Although it may have felt like a distraction for me, that moment on Wilshire Boulevard was a divine interruption. And ultimately, it became so much more.

## Defining Moments

The day I read the headline about the water crisis and allowed it to move me to do research became a defining moment in determining, expanding, and directing my dream. My God-dream was to be a pastor, to help people meet Jesus and change the world for His kingdom. But God used the divine interruption to expand His dream for me, enlarging it to include a role in helping people around the world gain access to clean drinking water. It's difficult for people to hear the good news of Jesus Christ when they're worried about basic survival needs. Jesus understood that. Over and over Jesus performed miracles of multiplying food and drink so that people could have their physical needs cared for, which then opened them to hearing about their spiritual needs.

That's what God did for my dream. He took that defining moment to show me what I could do to care for people in a more practical way. I thought my life focus was just on the local church I was leading, but I began to see how God had bigger plans. He wanted me to inspire people to reach around the world and demonstrate our faith by addressing not just spiritual needs but physical ones as well. I felt it was important to reach out to people and earn the right to talk to them about what motivates me to invest so much of myself in them. That's where Christ's amazing love comes into the conversation.

What I initially thought was a distraction, I later recognized as a divine interruption. As I continued to pursue the dream and see where God was leading me, I discovered that it had also become a defining moment.

But what about when we think something is a defining moment but it brings only disappointment?

## Turning Disappointments into Defining Moments

On January 22, 2010, talk-show host Conan O'Brien gave his farewell speech to *The Tonight Show* audience after more than twenty years with NBC. Only seven months into his time as the show's host, executives at NBC decided to make changes and approached Conan with two options: host an hour-long show in the 12:05 a.m. time slot, or leave the network. Conan chose to leave.

Opinions flew around about how NBC treated Conan, and people speculated as to whether he even had a choice in the matter. The media frenzy continued to escalate as the final show quickly approached. Fans were angry with NBC and protested, thinking the network was being unfair to Conan and his loyal viewers.

With tensions at an all-time high, in the last few minutes of the show, Conan gave his farewell address:

> Tonight I'm allowed to say anything I want. . . . I am enormously
> proud of the work we've done together, and I want to thank NBC
> for making it all possible. . . . To all the people watching, I can never
> ever thank you enough for the kindness to me. . . . All I ask is one
> thing . . . : please do not be cynical. . . . Nobody in life gets exactly
> what they thought they were going to get. But if you work really hard
> and you're kind, amazing things will happen.[8]

In a moment when he could say whatever he wanted, we find a man praising and supporting the very organization that was letting him go. Conan's approach is an example of how our circumstances do not have to dictate our responses. He took a disappointment and turned it into a defining moment. His determination to let go of the past and focus on the future freed him to pursue the next chapter of his dream.

We may not be able to choose what is dealt to us in life, but we are able to choose how we respond. Even though Conan was sincere in his comments, it was not easy for him. Although he may have felt hurt and mistreated, he did not allow his emotions to control his response. He didn't write off NBC and his season there based on what was currently happening. He looked back over his twenty years with the company, and with that perspective he allowed his tenure and experience, not his termination, to shape how he moved forward.

Perspective in difficult circumstances comes from stepping back and evaluating from a long-term point of view. When we encounter situations that make us feel as though we've been interrupted, distracted, or even derailed—such as what Conan experienced in losing what he thought was his dream job—we actually are presented with the opportunity to show our confidence in God, our trust that He is involved in our lives and that He is guiding us, whether we recognize it or not.

Gratitude is the secret that navigates us through difficult circumstances with our faith intact. Disappointments viewed through the lens of gratitude become defining moments because we are able to see something heartbreaking as an opportunity for growth, as a chance for a new direction. If we get stuck in our disappointment, we may remain focused on the closed door and miss the opened window. Without gratitude it is difficult to look at a situation that went sideways and to glean lessons from it. With gratitude we can discover a lot about ourselves, our motivations, and our methods. And in those times we can create defining moments.

Conan looked at his seven months in that role as an opportunity, not a right. Therefore, when asked to leave, though he was upset, he didn't treat it as an injustice. Gratitude, not entitlement, was the perspective he adopted to move past that obstacle. He focused not on what he had lost but on the opportunity he'd been given, and he was able to respond well.

We are going to face challenges. Sometimes they may just be small distractions that disrupt our focus. Sometimes the challenge may be a bigger interruption that completely changes our focus. And sometimes it may be a disappointment that offers an opportunity to refocus. Not all distractions will be useful, but it is important not to allow frustration and aggravation to take over and get us off track.

Unlock your dream by searching for God's wisdom to know the difference between a distraction and a divine interruption. Look for God in the interruption. He may be changing up your routines to shift your focus to something He wants you to do, some opportunity He doesn't want you to miss. And as you pursue those things, you will find that God presents defining moments that are true keys to unlocking your God-dream.

| | |

**DREAM LOCKS:** Distractions that can disrupt your dream are everywhere, and it can be hard to tell when a distraction is actually an interruption from God's hand to your heart.

**DREAM KEY:** Be alert and open to recognizing an opportunity instead of dismissing it as a distraction. What may feel like a disappointment or a derailment can actually be God redirecting you.

**SCRIPTURE KEY:** In their hearts humans plan their course, but the LORD establishes their steps. (Proverbs 16:9)

# If You Build It, He Will Come

> RAY KINSELLA: "If you build it, he will come."
> ANNIE KINSELLA: If you build what, who will come?
> RAY KINSELLA: He didn't say.
>
> —*Field of Dreams*

An important element of unlocking a God-dream is understanding that we won't be able to accomplish what we are meant to do in our strength alone; it will be beyond our ability to complete—and God designed it to be that way. We need to trust that God will guide us, open doors for us, and empower us with the ability to reach that dream. We will have to trust that He will bring others to join us along the way who will be instrumental in helping us to reach that dream.

Another part of following God's guidance is that we will often need to take risks in ways that may not seem reasonable. That is the faith part of our journey.

Do you have the courage to wade into risk and uncertainty? If you were considering venturing out on your own, without any guidance or resources, into something that was dangerous or untested, I wouldn't encourage you to do that. I am talking about stepping out in faith *with God,* and that's an adventure on a whole 'notha level!

When God leads you toward your dream, you will face things that don't seem humanly possible. But don't let that stop you, because He is in the business of doing things far greater than we can fathom. What may seem like risk to us is business as usual to God.

When we are willing to take risks, we make room for God to work. We are trusting Him and His ability to work miracles. Through our process of preparing for something amazing, something amazing begins to happen in us. But that happens only when we become willing to take the risk of trusting God.

## What Keeps Us from Risking?

Plenty of things can keep us from taking appropriate risks—doubt, fear, a lack of resources—and can prevent us from realizing all that God has for us. These obstacles to faith are some of the biggest dream killers. They also eat away at our relationship with God.

The criticisms we face as we pursue our dreams can create doubt. If we listen to our critics, we begin to doubt ourselves and the direction God has given us. At times God will lead us on a path that makes sense only to a few other people. Many might question what you are considering, but as long as you know you are where God wants you and you have support from respected leaders, you have to take that risk. Don't let the fear of criticism, or not knowing exactly how everything will work out, make you abandon your dream.

> *What may seem like risk to us is business as usual to God.*

Fear can completely disable your dream if you allow it to take root. Some fear is normal, but you can't allow it to paralyze you. It is one thing to hesitate in pursuing your dream to become a lion tamer or a stunt driver because of the danger involved; it is another issue to avoid stepping into the dream of leading a company or becoming a pastor because you are afraid of public speaking. Let fear make you cautious as you move forward, give you pause to reassess, or wisdom to protect yourself. Don't let fear paralyze you and keep you from moving forward with your dream. Feel the fear and do it anyway.

It's hard enough to go after a dream when you face doubt and fear, but a lack of resources is a major obstacle that makes any risk feel even more insurmountable. Drawing on your already-limited existing resources of time, money, or security to pursue a dream may sound like a ridiculous move. The only way to overcome this barrier is to trust God to provide for you and to provide a way for you to accomplish what He calls you to do.

Doubt, fear, criticism, and a lack of resources—all of these will make the risks you encounter feel bigger than they should. Trusting in the power and might of God is the only way to move past those obstacles to realize your dreams.

## A Risky Lesson in Faith

After I spent a few years as a pastor, one of my dreams became to find a church building—our own home, a place where we could do our work and allow for more growth in our ministry. During the first seventeen years our church existed, we met in eighteen different locations. We rented or leased what we could find or afford, everything from schoolrooms to community centers to storefronts.

But we never stopped dreaming or looking. Finally, in 1997 we found an old art deco movie theater for sale. It needed a lot of work, but we thought this would be a great home. The only problem was that it was way out of our price range: the building was worth about two million dollars. We were a small church, inexperienced in business dealings. But we had a dream. The more we prayed, the more we felt God leading us to take the risk.

We made an outrageously low offer, along with a meager ten-thousand-dollar down payment. We thought no owner in her right mind would accept our offer. But we had a dream that God was asking us to take a risk on, so we made it. And the owner, a retired woman who was eager to sell, agreed on the price!

When I heard the news, I felt like walking into a room with our leadership team, closing the door, and laughing about how crazy it felt that someone trusted us enough to sell it to us. At the same time, though, we knew we could handle it, because we trusted God. If He was leading us to take this risk, then we knew He would be faithful to see it to completion.

The building, named the Four Star Theater, had an impressive history. The "four stars" were for the founders of United Artists: Charlie Chaplin, Douglas Fairbanks, Mary Pickford, and D. W. Griffith. Major movie premieres—with the giant spotlights shooting into the night sky and with Hollywood's elite attending—had played there, such as *Lost Horizon* in 1937, *The Grapes of Wrath* in 1940, and *Julius Caesar* in 1953. *Gone with the Wind* was screened there for the press three days before its grand opening.

Later it became a place to see obscure movies, indie films, and foreign films. After that it became a porn theater, and finally it was a place to see second- and third-run movies for a dollar. Then we bought it, and it became a church, a place for lives to be redeemed and transformed, a place to take friends who needed to discover Jesus.

We loved our home, our community, and the exciting ministry we were experiencing. We thought our dream had been fulfilled. For seventeen years we saw people's lives changed, marriages healed, broken hearts repaired, and dreams inspired. Story after story unfolded in that old theater. We saw teenagers come to a life of faith free from drug addiction. We had twentysomethings who had moved to Hollywood to pursue their dreams and were now following Christ or even going into ministry.

It was awesome! But within several years, we outgrew the building. The parking was always a problem, we had maxed out the children's ministry area, and we held four and sometimes five services on a weekend just to accommodate everyone. We realized God wasn't yet finished with His dream for us; we needed to find another building so we could continue to reach new people and serve those who already attended. We began looking for a larger home. In Los Angeles anything we could find that had the right zoning and parking cost between twenty-five and thirty *million* dollars—*way* out of our league.

For the next seven years we looked.

At times I had to resist my doubts. I wondered if God was going to lead us to a new home or not. If He did, how would He provide the resources we needed? What if we found a place and then, after we moved in, we couldn't afford it? I worried about all the details of taking this kind of risk.

What was happening to our dream? We were ready to take a risk, but where was God? Why hadn't He shown us the next step? Was this dream really His desire for us?

Eventually, we stopped actively looking.

The process of finding a possible location, looking at it, asking questions, beginning to dream about it, and getting our hopes up only to realize this was another building that would not work was frustrating and disheartening. That process was also a distraction to the work we were doing in our existing location. We had people who needed our ministry right then.

One day I received a phone call from the real-estate agent we'd been working with. "An old church built in 1927 just listed," he told me. "They haven't even put For Sale signs up yet. Do you want to go see it?"

By this point, we had seen so many buildings it was hard to muster any enthusiasm about another one. But I agreed, inwardly sighing and not expecting much.

When we pulled up to the building, I was stunned. This wasn't a church; it was a cathedral! The picturesque style was designed by the famous architect Robert H. Orr. It also had a huge stained-glass window portrait of a rose, a replica of the one at the Reims Cathedral in France.

The sign on the outside read Wilshire Christian Church. It was listed for eight million dollars.

*Also out of our league,* I thought when I heard the amount.

The agent explained that the city of Los Angeles had designated the cathedral as a historic landmark. This kept real-estate developers from tearing it down to build an office or condo high-rise. Only a church or some kind of museum could buy it. This kept the price "low enough" so we could consider trying to buy it.

My mind raced back and forth between *This is a great building* and *This will never work for us* as we walked through. It was a little farther toward downtown than I had wanted to move, but the building looked amazing. Though the neighborhood's vibe was really different from our current home, I thought the community could be a cool place for our church. But it looked like a cathedral. Would younger people in our congregation like the more traditional style? Even with all these concerns, I knew in my heart that this was it! But how would we ever afford it, even at the "steal" everyone claimed it was?

I tried not to get my hopes up. But then I remembered that God had given me His dream, that if this really was to be our church's new home, then He would be faithful. Still I wondered, *Will He come through this time?* I mean, this was a risk of enormous proportions. Was I ready to take that kind of risk, even for a God-dream?

As I viewed this beautiful church, an unusual movie slipped into my mind.

## The Field of Dreams

In 1989 Kevin Costner starred in a runaway hit called *Field of Dreams*. When I first saw it, I thought it was one of the weirdest movies I'd ever seen. My wife, Holly, and I kept looking at each other and whispering, "What's going on now?" But it was about baseball, and I'm a huge baseball fan, so we kept watching.

The story goes that while working in his cornfield, a novice farmer, Ray Kinsella (played by Costner) hears a voice that whispers, "If you build it, he will come." That's followed by a vision of a baseball diamond in the middle of his cornfield.

After wrestling with the meaning of the voice and the vision, he decides to take the risk and build the field. Ray explains to his wife that he wants to follow the instructions because he does not want to be like his father, an unhappy man who was unable to act on his dreams. His dad had experienced an unsuccessful baseball career and pushed Ray to become a ballplayer in an attempt to impose on his son the dream he'd had to abandon.

When Ray was about seventeen, they'd argued and he'd said some hurtful things to his father. To Ray's regret, they never repaired the relationship before his father died. He believes that somehow this vision is his last chance to pursue a dream and be different from his dad. So he plows up a big part of his cornfield, destroying potential crops for his income, and builds a baseball field. Then . . . nothing happens.

Ray soon faces financial ruin because of the crops sacrificed to this endeavor, and people begin to pressure him to sell the farm.

One night, however, a man in an old-fashioned baseball uniform appears on the field. It's "Shoeless" Joe Jackson, a baseball player who had died a few decades earlier but whom Ray's father had idolized. Shoeless Joe is thrilled to play baseball again, because he had been banned from playing; he had been convicted of helping to throw the 1919 World Series and had finished his life with this regret.

Later, other players also unable to live out their baseball-playing dreams show up on Ray's field. They play baseball, and at the end of each day, the players disappear into the cornfield as if it were a doorway back into some mysterious realm of eternity.

But it isn't just professional ballplayers who show up. Other characters—a famous author who once loved baseball and a doctor who left his dream of playing after only one game to pursue a medical career—enter the story, each of whom had a dream that was interrupted, then abandoned for one reason or another. Both are recruited into Ray's unclear yet compelling vision. The author encourages Ray by telling him, "People will come, Ray. People will come" to relive their childhood innocence and revisit their dreams.

In one of the final scenes, Ray has become discouraged because he thinks that his "field of dreams" was fun but he just isn't sure what the reason is. Shoeless Joe challenges Ray's thinking and then shows him why Ray sacrificed so much. "If you build it, *he* will come," Joe says as he draws Ray's attention toward home plate.

The catcher standing there removes his mask. Ray recognizes this young man. It's his father, a much younger version. As his father heads toward the cornfield at the end of the game, Ray asks him to play catch. It becomes clear that the "he" of "he will come" is Ray's dad, a man just like Ray, a man with dreams and real-life heartbreaks that he had to navigate the best way he knew how. The other "he" who arrives is the *version of Ray* who needed to emerge in order to enjoy the fulfillment of his dream. As they begin to play catch, the picture broadens to reveal hundreds of cars, lined up for miles, approaching the field.

In the end, people gather to have another chance to reach their dreams. Some left dreams behind because of other pursuits, some because of mistakes they made, others because circumstances took the opportunities from them. Here's the scene as Ray walks on the baseball field with his dad:

JOHN KINSELLA: Is this heaven?

RAY KINSELLA: It's Iowa.

JOHN: Iowa. I could've sworn this was heaven.

RAY: Is there a heaven?

JOHN: Oh yeah . . . Heaven's where dreams come true.

RAY: [Ray looks toward the house and sees his wife and daughter on the veranda.] Then maybe this is heaven.

## If You Build It, He Will Come

As I stood in that cathedral, I reflected on that movie, Ray's vision, and the story of his journey. It had meaning for me as well.

*If you build it*, He *will come.*

We weren't building a baseball diamond in a cornfield, but we needed a faith just as risky and strong. Just as Ray Kinsella risked everything he owned on a dream, I knew that God was asking us to do the same. We had to step out, to believe, to act, and to have faith. We had to swallow our fears and doubts, then make a move. And God would show up.

After three months negotiating on the price, I received a call one night from our real-estate agent.

"I got a phone call from the church's agent with a verbal approval for your offer of $7.6 million. They will send over the signed agreement in the morning."

"So it's a done deal? A verbal agreement is solid?" I asked.

"Yes, it's good. Congratulations."

We were so excited, Holly and I were high-fiving each other. We weren't sure how we were going to get that money, but we trusted that we would. Nothing could bring us down.

Until I got another call the next morning.

"The paperwork didn't get delivered," the agent told me apologetically. "I called to ask when I could expect it. They said they've decided to take an offer from another church."

I wasn't sure I'd heard him correctly. "Another church? Wait. How is that possible? We're the only buyer they've talked to for the last three months. I thought we had a verbal agreement. I thought that was binding."

"An offer came in late last night, and they've decided to take that one instead. It's not illegal, but it is highly unethical. I've been on the phone with them for a while, but they won't budge. I've been in commercial real estate for twenty years and I've never had this happen before."

"Why don't they want to consider another offer from us? Can't we do anything?"

"We can submit another offer right away. We can raise the amount. The other agent is legally obligated to show it to his clients."

*Raise the amount?* We had already stretched beyond a comfortable level.

After the church board and I discussed our options and prayed about it, I took a deep breath as we decided to trust that God was in fact leading us to this church building as our new home. So we raised our offer amount again and resubmitted it.

The new amount was enough to get their attention and to bring us back into the conversation, so they let us know that they would set a date for a "closed-bid offer." In thirty days they wanted both interested buyers to make a personal appearance before their board of directors, make a presentation of our plans, and bring our best and final offers.

*Great,* I thought. *We've made our best and final offer twice already. Now I need to come up with one more "final" offer.*

I couldn't figure out which church in LA was all of a sudden trying to buy this building. If I just knew who it was, I could talk to them. I prayed, *God, show me what You want me to do. I believe You want us to have this building. If You show me who is trying to buy it, I'll go talk to them.*

A week later, I got a call from one of our church members who often speaks at churches around the country. She said, "A couple days ago I was speaking at a church in another state, and afterward we went out to eat with the pastoral team. At dinner the pastor who heard I was from the Los Angeles area remarked that they had just put an offer on a church building near Wilshire and Normandie because they wanted to start a new congregation in Southern California. I didn't say anything, but they must be the ones bidding against us."

I spoke with a couple of pastor friends whom I often go to for advice. They encouraged me to contact the buyers and just tell them our story. I wanted to let them know about our longevity here in LA. I thought maybe they did not know they were stepping into a deal already in progress. Maybe putting a voice and a face to the other buyer could help them understand the situation. So I made a phone call.

Although I could not reach the senior pastor, the executive pastor returned my call.

"I think it's great that you want to start a church here in LA," I told him. "We need more churches. I just wanted you to know a little of our story, from one pastor to another. We've been here for more than twenty-five years, and this would really help us grow our church to the next level. We have already been in negotiations for three months, and your offer came as a surprise. They had already agreed to sell it to us. I wanted to ask if you would prayerfully consider removing your offer so we could continue with the purchase we started. We would be so grateful and would be willing to help you find another building that is smaller, since you would be just starting."

When he responded, his voice was tense. He informed me that they would *not* remove their offer, that they had a huge mailing list of people in the LA area who bought their pastor's books and listened to his podcasts, and they planned on starting with two thousand people on their first Sunday. "Since it's taken you twenty-five years and you are only now reaching two thousand people, and we can start with that on day one, maybe you should remove *your* offer and let us get the building. We can do a better job reaching people than you have."

I was stunned. So much for the pastors' heart-to-heart talk. I tried again. "I'm sorry, I must not have communicated very well in what I was trying to say. I'm not challenging you or saying you shouldn't come to LA. I'm just trying to explain our situation and wanted you to consider that."

"I understood you. And we are not taking back the offer. We are going to get the building. You should just let it go. We've raised $7.8 million for this, and we are going to buy it with all cash."

"Oh. Okay. Well, that's way more than we have; we can't compete with that amount. But I appreciate your listening to me. I guess I'll see you when we make our final offers." I hung up the phone, disappointed and confused about why this was happening and if this was actually a God-dream.

We didn't have that kind of money. We were outmatched. Then I realized, *Wait, did he just tell me how much their offer is going to be?*

I talked with our staff pastors, leaders, and friends. Should we raise our offer another two hundred thousand? Should we raise it three hundred thousand? What if we were off by fifty thousand? Did I misunderstand what he was saying? Maybe they'd up their offer one or two hundred thousand, but I was not going to try to guess and risk losing it. I didn't want to lose the building and look back and think, *If I had only offered two hundred thousand more than I did, we could have had the building.*

"What do we do, God?" I prayed. "You've brought us this far. Now what?"

I felt God whisper into my heart, *Offer $9 million.*

I just about choked. Nine million! That *would* take a miracle!

"God, we don't have nine million. How are we going to do that?"

It may have just been me, but I think I heard the Holy Spirit reply, *You don't have $7.6 million either, so you just have to trust Me with this amount too.*

"Good point," I conceded.

I felt a little like Peter walking on the water and suddenly looking at the storm around him and saying, "Wait a minute, Jesus. I can't walk on water during a storm!" And Jesus replying, "Peter, you can't walk on water at any time! Just keep looking at Me. That's the point here. Keep looking at Me and fear not."

God was asking me to take a huge risk. And I could only take it by trusting that He would see me through it.

When the day came to make our offer, we prepared a presentation with video and photos and told stories of what we wanted to do in that building. We told the sellers, "We know that you have spent the last eighty years in this building ministering to people in Los Angeles. We honor you for your work here, and we ask you to trust us to build on the work you have already done so we continue to reach the people here." Then we offered nine million for the building.

They accepted our offer!

We were so excited. God had done a miracle. But the failed attempt by the other potential buyers cost us an additional $1.4 million.

That stung.

We now faced the task of raising money to close escrow. We needed $2.5 million.

No problem.

"God," I prayed, "thank You so much for letting us get the deal. We are so grateful. Now as I'm sure You've noticed, we need $2.5 million to close escrow. God, we don't have $2.5 million. Where are we going to get it? I mean, I know *You* have $2.5 million, Lord. But we don't." I took a deep breath and continued. "I believe You are leading us to get this building, so I trust that You will provide what we need."

We really had no previous experience in real-estate acquisitions that would give us enough swag to pursue a property like this, but we dared to dream a God-sized dream and then step out to take the risk and chase it. It seems strange to say this now, because I have worried about a lot smaller needs than this one, but I stopped worrying about the money. God gave me a simple confidence to trust Him for this one.

I remembered the first building we bought years ago. In the 1990s our worship leader at the time, Tyrone Williams, had just finished leading worship at a conference in the Baltimore area. When he returned he told me that one of the speakers, Dr. Charles Dixon from Ghana, West Africa, had given him a prophetic word for me. A prophetic word is an encouraging message, often accentuated with Scripture, prayer, and statements about God's desire for the person being spoken to. Sometimes these words are general, sometimes they come with requirements for the listener, and sometimes they contain specific pieces of information to clarify that it's the Holy Spirit inspiring the message. This particular message contained amazingly specific information, but it also led to more than I realized.

The message had been recorded on a cassette tape.*

"I have a word for your pastor. I see he is kind of like a . . . white pastor?" Dixon asked. (Yes, he was correct about that part.)

"Is his name Philip?" (Okay, that was two. A white guy named Philip.) "God is going to give him a theater for the church. The church is going to be racially diverse. There will be young people who are not being reached by others. God is going to use him in Africa, Mexico, Caribbean, and other nations." (Many of the things he prophesied have happened over the years.)

As we faced this new challenge of raising $2.5 million, I thought that if

---

* If you are under twenty years old, a *cassette tape* is a plastic rectangle, about the size of your cell phone, and has magnetic tape inside with sound recordings on it.

I played that recording for some of our leaders, it would inspire them to know that God had led us and provided for us before, and that He would lead us and provide for us this time.

I searched in my garage and dug up the old cassette recording and a cassette player.* I also found a second recording. Dr. Dixon had come to visit us after we had received that first message, and he had spoken another prophetic word that we recorded. I decided to listen to both because it had been about ten years since I had heard them. As I listened to the second tape, I heard something I had never paid attention to before. I guess the first time around I was so excited that we were going to move into the theater, our first home (which we did), and that he knew I was a white guy named Philip (which I am), that I didn't pay much attention to the other parts of his message.

On that second recording Dixon said something that froze me right where I stood. I felt God had led me to this moment to speak to me or, more precisely, to remind me that He had *already* spoken to me.

Dr. Dixon said, "Don't worry about the money. This is the *first* transition, and in the *next transition* I am releasing $2.5 million to you so you can build the ministry."

Chill bumps popped up on my neck.

There it was, a message given to me several years earlier that would bring encouragement and faith to believe God for the miracles we knew we needed for this dream to come true.

The "first transition" was getting the Four Star Theater, and the "second transition" was the cathedral. God was letting us know that He knew how much we would need and that He was taking care of it.

The next day I took the tape and player to our staff meeting and played it for them. I was laughing and crying. They were so pumped!

We began to pray and tell the people in our church about the need. We

---

\* If you are under twenty years old, a *cassette player* is a device that you put a cassette into and listen to what was recorded on the magnetic tape.

held a prayer walk and mapped out an area, one mile in every direction, around the cathedral's neighborhood. As we walked we lifted up the people who lived in that community. We laid our hands on the building itself and asked for God's blessing and provision. I drove alone to the building many times and prayed for it and for our future neighbors.

Church members, friends, other churches, even people I'd never met gave money. Almost every week someone I did not expect would give ten or twenty or even fifty thousand dollars. One church donated one hundred thousand dollars for our building fund.

The week before the money was due, we still needed two hundred fifty thousand dollars to complete the full $2.5 million that we needed. I'd felt so confident because of the speed at which the money poured in. But as we got down to the wire, I began to wonder if we would actually reach the full amount.

At the eleventh hour a couple in our church gave us stock to sell to use toward the down payment. When the stock was sold, the total amount was three hundred thousand dollars. God had proved faithful.

## A Good Risk Versus a Bad Risk

Whenever I tell this story, inevitably the question comes up: How do I know if it's a good risk to take or an unwise one? After all, risking millions of dollars without knowing you have God's clear direction can be catastrophic—not just for your dreams but also for your life and quite possibly the lives of those you're closest to. So how do you know when to take a risk and whether it's the right risk?

The first thing you need to do in any circumstance is to pray. Our guidance and reassurance of that direction should come through prayer.

Also talk to trusted advisors and experts who share your faith and have more knowledge, experience, and training in a specific field to help you in your decisions. If it's a real-estate deal, for instance, talk to someone who is in the business and can help you avoid pitfalls and navigate the process. If it is a legal issue, go to an attorney who can advise you on how to handle the contract, lawsuit, or regulations you face, and then consider it from a biblical perspective.

Everything in life holds unknowns you can't predict, which is when faith, discernment, and wisdom play a big role, but you don't have to figure it out alone. Your network of relationships can help you mitigate a lot of the risk that comes from your inexperience or lack of knowledge.

## Step Out and See How God Responds

Your dream may not involve needing millions of dollars. But it will take a million-dollar level of trust and risk. Don't allow doubt, fear, a lack of resources, or constantly playing the "what if" game to keep you from the dream God has placed in your heart.

When we allow ourselves to take risks, we open ourselves to God's miraculous, awe-inspiring work. He is eager to show us what He can do in and through our needs. When the church community and I were in need, we could have allowed fear to keep us from going where we thought God was leading, but we clung to the hope that comes from knowing God is in it with us.

You will face challenges as you pursue your God-dream. Don't let fears and doubts keep you from realizing your full potential. Playing off what they said in *Field of Dreams,* you can trust that if God has given you a message and if you build it, He will come. If you step out in faith and take a risk, He will show up and do miraculous things. He will be there to help you fulfill what He intends for you to do.

||

**DREAM LOCK:** Doubt, fear, or lack of resources will be the most common barriers to pursuing your God-dream.

**DREAM KEY:** The only way past these barriers is to pray, talk to strong advisors, and then step out and see what God does and where He takes you.

**SCRIPTURE KEY:** Have I not commanded you? Be strong and courageous. Do not be frightened, and do not be dismayed, for the LORD your God is with you wherever you go. (Joshua 1:9, ESV)

# Finding Your Way in a Desert

Have you ever had that feeling that this is the best I'm
ever gonna do, this is the best I'm ever gonna feel . . .
and it ain't that great?

—MITCH ROBBINS, *City Slickers*

When I first moved to Los Angeles, I started attending the Vineyard Christian Fellowship in West LA and soon made friends with Al Kasha, a Jewish
man who had put his faith in Christ as his Messiah. He was passionate about
his faith and an inspiration to me. He was also a Hollywood success: he had
won two Academy Awards and had written many Top 40 hits, movie scores,
and even a song for Elvis.

Al hosted Bible studies in his home. I met a lot of interesting people there,
including Bob Dylan. Al and I spent a lot of time together praying and listening to recordings of great Bible teachers. He was like an older brother to me.

One day several years into our friendship, Al asked if I would teach a
Bible study at his home. I accepted, excited but nervous since this was my first
time to lead a study like this. Only ten people attended that first evening.
Considering Al's other Bible studies were often crammed with people, I felt
let down. But I was determined to stick it out.

Soon the Bible study began to grow, and before long we were packing
more than sixty people into his living room. A lot of celebrities attended during those early Bible studies—Donna Summer, Debbie Boone, Nell Carter,

Jerome Anthony of Little Anthony and the Imperials. Music producers, show-business people, and entertainment hopefuls all filled the house. On a couple of occasions I had to ask that people not bring their demo tapes, eight-by-ten photos, and bios to the Bible study, since it wasn't supposed to be a place for career networking.

After a few months, I felt God expand my dream when He whispered into my heart to start a church. It would be a place where people could have a genuine experience with the living Jesus. Beyond that, I wasn't too clear about what the church would look like. But one day as I was reading in the book of Isaiah, I saw these two passages:

> Do not remember the former things,
> Nor consider the things of old.
> Behold, I will do a new thing,
> Now it shall spring forth;
> Shall you not know it?
> I will even make a road in the wilderness
> And rivers in the desert.[1]

> Then the eyes of the blind shall be opened,
> And the ears of the deaf shall be unstopped.
> Then the lame shall leap like a deer,
> And the tongue of the dumb sing.
> For waters shall burst forth in the wilderness,
> And streams in the desert.
> The parched ground shall become a pool,
> And the thirsty land springs of water.[2]

That's when I saw more clearly the church I wanted to lead. I love the local church. I believe it is the hope of the world. Throughout my life I have experienced God's presence and heard the good news of Jesus Christ in churches, and that has affected me deeply. It has also marked what I dream about. I've also been in churches that were judgmental and self-righteous. They focused on certain aspects of life that seem like minor issues and not the major priorities that Jesus calls us to.

It bothered me to know that some people had been so wounded by their experiences in local churches that they no longer felt comfortable enough to attend. In this desert—with the lack of positive church experiences and the lack of genuine familiarity with the living Jesus—people needed an oasis. They needed a place where they could find healing, inspiration, direction, compassion, and genuine faith. I wanted to lead people who might be uncomfortable in a typical church but who could enjoy an atmosphere that was different from what they had previously experienced, an atmosphere that was encouraging and refreshing. I wanted to lead the kind of church that would allow people to give Jesus another try. (Of course, it's not really Jesus whom they were giving another try, but His followers.)

Sometimes our dissatisfaction with the norm prompts us to dream of what could be. To me, I saw a spiritual desert in Los Angeles, so an "oasis" seemed like the answer. I dreamed of leading a church where people could find love and acceptance, where their faith in Jesus could flourish and change the quality of their lives. So with Al's encouragement, along with the blessing and support of my then-fiancée, Holly, and many friends, I decided to pursue that dream. I had big goals for this new church, and I believed that because God had given me the dream, He had big goals for it as well. And in April 1984, the Oasis Church began.

## Not Quite What I Was Expecting

We did not start the Bible study originally with the thought of launching a new church. I realized that many of the people who attended the Bible study already had a church. I knew that many of those people would not join me in our new endeavor. However, I really underestimated the attraction of the "Hollywood scene" environment. It never occurred to me that Al's Oscars displayed on the mantle behind me and the presence of celebrities might have been driving some of the Bible study's success. I overestimated the attraction of my teaching.

On the first Sunday we had sixty people. I learned later that many of those were friends who simply wanted to show their support on day one. The next Sunday we had thirty-five people. The Sunday after that, the number shrank to twenty-four. I spent the next week fearful that no one would show up the following Sunday. Hello, discouragement.

After two months, our worship leader and his wife, along with three singers they'd brought with them to help, left for another church. Five down, nineteen to go. I became the pastor *and* the worship leader. Discouragement hit on a whole 'notha level.

We were growing in the wrong direction. People stayed *away* by the thousands. We remained a small church for a very long time. I figured that at the current rate, it would be only a matter of weeks before it was down to Holly and me on a Sunday morning. The church service would become sort of a Sunday-morning *date.* And that's not romantic.

People kept telling me, "Your church has so much potential."

Their words didn't offer much encouragement, and after a while I began to think, *Oy vey! Everything has potential! The Chicago Cubs have potential.* * *Dying plants have potential. What else could we have* but *potential?*

Have you ever felt that way?

It can be frustrating to work hard at your dream while the result remains consistent: "One day you may be good at this." Many dreamers work really hard to find only small elements of progress. This is when the input and sup-

---

* At the time, the Cubs were at the bottom of the standings, but as I write this book, they have become a contending team. We'll see if they realize *their* dream.

port of mentors have a big impact. They can be essential for helping you figure out the steps to take for moving past where you are stuck. (I'll talk more about this later.)

For some reason I can't recall, we initially started meeting in a school in Encino rather than in LA where we belonged. To get to the school, we drove up a street named Hayvenhurst, right past the large gated home of Michael Jackson. Many days a small crowd of people waited outside the gate hoping to get a glimpse of Michael.

One Sunday after a service that had just a few more people in attendance than are allowed on an NBA roster, I noticed there were more people standing outside Michael Jackson's house than had come to our church. I could do better standing *there* conducting a service with those people than we were doing in our school building.

As I drove past, I thought, *Someone just shoot me and say it was an accident.*

When we arrived home, I dropped off my now-wife, Holly, and stayed in the car. "I'm going for a drive," I said with clear despair.

"Are you okay? Where are you going?" Holly asked.

"I'm either going to commit a random misdemeanor or go out for ice cream. I'll decide on the drive." #OverlyDramatic.

It felt as if the whole dream were one big mistake. I believed that God had given me that dream, but with each passing week in which no new people showed up, I began to second-guess myself and what I felt God had led me into. I felt lost and was plagued by uncertainty.

We had no one to help us start our church, no guidance, no mentor, and we did so many things wrong. We had the wrong location, the wrong approach, no clear vision. My sermons were too long. The services were too long. Our praise and worship was weak. Our offerings were low. I had no idea how to train leaders, and I didn't know how to build a team. I had no target audience. I was afraid that if I chose a certain group to target, I might leave some people out, and I needed all the people I could find. Other than these few minor issues, we were doing great!

Holly and I had started the church in April and got married eight months later. A new church and a new marriage at the same time made both much harder than they needed to be. This was not a great strategy. While trying to grow our church, I had to keep a regular job too. For a while I worked at a computer-software company. I even drove a limo for three months. I'll never know how I found the customers' destinations in the days before a GPS, since I am directionally challenged even on a good day.

Starting a church was a lot harder than I expected. Many of our projects and efforts just did not work. But I tried to take the high road. "Well, that didn't end the way I expected, but at least no one died," I often reminded myself.

The visions of success I'd held on to seemed to shrink in the reality of each Sunday. Had I misheard God? Was this *not* the dream I was supposed to pursue? *Should I quit?*

I wanted to do the right thing; I just wasn't sure what that was. I realized I needed help figuring out the answers to those questions.

## The Influence of Mentors

King Solomon's sage advice instructs us that "plans fail for lack of counsel, but with many advisers they succeed."[3] So I started to meet with pastors who were wise leaders. I sought their advice and leadership ideas and talked through frustrations and doubts. Each time, I walked away with the consistent message: persevere. They shared their own experiences of uncertainty and mistakes they'd made, then explained that with perseverance and continual commitment to grow in their own knowledge of leadership, they stuck it out and their dreams became a reality. But it took time. Those mentors reminded me that pursuing a God-dream doesn't guarantee overnight success. It takes work, faith, and a huge amount of perseverance.

As we pursue our dreams it can be easy to get lost in the goals we set for ourselves or to feel abandoned along the way if things don't work out as we thought they would. It is important to have mentors and guides to help us make the choices that lead where we want and need to go. The wise people who became my mentors reminded me that we can't give up when things don't immediately go our way. If I hadn't taken time to seek their advice, my dream was sure to fail. The same is true for the dream that feels as though it isn't on track with where you think it should be.

Knowing the right people who are willing to support you can make a huge difference in how you approach your dreams. They will see things objectively, encourage and challenge you, pray for and with you, and hold you accountable. I've discovered that the best way to find these people is by being connected to a local church community, where they will love and support you in figuring out your God-dream. It is also there that you will discover the greatest mentor and guide you could ever hope for: Jesus.

## The Importance of Perseverance

Armed with encouragement from various mentors, I went back to our small church and kept at it. People came and went. Mostly went. For five years I awoke early every Sunday morning in fear that no one would show up.

We moved venues. I prayed. I attended classes on church growth, leadership, and church structure at Fuller Theological Seminary. I also attended intensive classes like Breaking the 200 Barrier, which church growth and leadership experts C. Peter Wagner and John Maxwell taught.

I discovered the significance of Proverbs 24:3–4: "By wisdom a house is built, and through understanding it is established; through knowledge its rooms are filled with rare and beautiful treasures." Slowly I began to understand some of what I was missing in my leadership strategy, what we were doing wrong or what we were leaving out. And that's when I and our church began to change for the better.

> *Rarely will you encounter a road that is perfectly smooth. If you give up every time it gets bumpy, you'll never reach your dream.*

The important lesson of persevering revealed itself in my willingness to learn and try new ways to pursue my dream. I had to be willing to change, to grow, to adjust and readjust. In time, the church and I discovered more clearly who we were, what we were supposed to do, and whom we were supposed to reach. That's when the perseverance began to pay off and the dream began to solidify.

One of the best things I ever did was to keep at it. Problems came and went, people came and went, but I kept showing up. I kept praying, I kept believing, and some days when I didn't feel like I had a lot of faith, I kept working at it anyway.

If we want to unlock our dreams, we must be willing to persevere, to persist. Persistence—spiritual tenacity—is the ability that allows all other abilities to flourish in your life. Many times over the last thirty-two years I've wanted to quit—on Mondays after a Sunday with ministerial challenges or a weak service, on Wednesdays after difficulties I was trying to solve. I even wanted to quit once during a sermon that was falling flat. But I kept on working to build a church community and improve as a leader, and when I did, the struggles yielded rewards in strong relationships, healed wounds, and changed lives.

Rarely will you encounter a road that is perfectly smooth. If you give up every time it gets bumpy, you'll never reach your dream, and the only way to keep pressing toward it on rough roads is through perseverance.

## Learn to Laugh

When setbacks come, we need to keep ourselves energized enough to face them with faith. I used to think if we could just solve this or that problem, then ministry would become easier. I had to accept the reality that problems come up every week; it's a never-ending cycle. Leadership is problem solving. When we accept that as part of this journey—moving from problem to problem—we are less frustrated when the next challenge comes.

One thing that has helped me in pursuing my dreams is learning to laugh. Most of the time I find frustrating moments funnier the more time separates me from the event. And I'm still working on finding humor in the midst of the crisis. But it's important to lighten up.

In Proverbs we read, "A cheerful heart is good medicine, but a broken spirit saps a person's strength."[4] If we don't allow ourselves to find humor in situations and encourage our hearts to be lightened by laughter, then weariness is sure to overtake our dreams and drain us of the energy we need.

I admit that laughter was difficult to find in the middle of those lean years when Oasis was not yet the church we had dreamed of. The first few years of ministry were a lot of "it seemed like a good idea at the time" experiences strung together. Failure isn't all it's cracked up to be.

After a series of challenges that would discourage the most optimistic leader, I said to Holly, "If I weren't the pastor of this church, I wouldn't even attend here." That's a red flag when you don't want to attend the church you're leading.

"Everything rises and falls on leadership," John Maxwell has said. I've heard that statement and thought, *Oh great. My bad.*

After so much struggle and discouragement, we finally decided to at least have fun while building our church. We didn't change everything overnight. It was gradual but consistent. I stopped wearing a suit and tie and just wore what I was comfortable in: jeans. We changed our music to be more like what we would enjoy at home. We were more intentional about creating moments in our service when we could just laugh. I grew more relaxed and began to trust that Jesus was building His church, that I could do my part and let Him do His part. We loved people and enjoyed serving God together.

As we began to lighten up, our approach to church became more creative, and we connected more with people. We were talking about what people needed to hear. We were teaching the Bible in a way that pointed them toward the help and direction they needed. We stopped trying to answer questions that no one was asking. People wanted to know how the Bible could help them live better. People were getting saved. We began to grow our attendance from that point forward. Young people we were not reaching before started coming in larger numbers.

One Sunday after the service, a man came up. With a big smile, he said, "I really liked your . . . speech? Talk? What do you call it?"

" 'Sermon.' But 'talk' is fine. I know what you mean," I said.

"I liked it because you were honest and there was no B.S." (Although he didn't use the initials.)[5]

"Oh. Okay. Thank you. No one's ever said that to me before." (Not in those exact words.)

The more we were able to let go of being so serious all the time with our dream, the more we saw the benefits of what was really happening. Of course, we had many challenging times when it was difficult to see beyond the stress, when it was almost impossible to find anything worth laughing about. But we persevered. I realized that laughter and embracing a "lighten up" mentality puts things in a better perspective.

## Making Jesus Famous

The Hollywood sign, celebrity mansions, palm tree–lined streets, and the Hollywood Walk of Fame are some of the famous icons of our city. The Walk of Fame has about twenty-five hundred stars placed in the sidewalk as monuments to the achievements of actors, musicians, directors, producers, writers, and others in the entertainment industry. Every year millions of people visit those stars.

What many people don't realize is that there is also a Friends of the Walk of Fame. These stars recognize the various contributions of other special honorees, such as the Los Angeles Dodgers, Magic Johnson, and the Apollo 11 astronauts: Neil Armstrong, Edwin Aldrin Jr., and Michael Collins.

> *You may say that I'm a dreamer.*
> *But I'm not the only one.*
> —John Lennon, "Imagine"

When we bought the Four Star Theater on Wilshire Boulevard, I loved the idea of church in a theater. Part of the significance of every theater in Los Angeles is that someone—a great actor, singer, or director—became famous either there or after getting his or her start there. Our purpose was to make Jesus famous, so we decided to make a star for Him and install it in the sidewalk in front of our theater. Who would make a better Friend of the Walk of Fame?

In 1998, we contracted with the company who made the stars for the Walk of Fame to make a star for us with the design we provided. It read *Jesus Christ* inside the star and *the Son of God* below it. While the other stars had an icon of a movie camera, radio microphone, or record/CD, we designed our icon with an open Bible and a sword lying across the pages. We chose that icon because the Bible is described as the "sword of the Spirit" and Scripture describes Jesus as "the Word became human and made his home among us."[6]

I wanted to create a special event to unveil the star just as they do for celebrities. After a few months of planning, we had the star installed and covered so no one could see it until the unveiling. We hired a publicist to get the news out to the media and enlisted the help of several church members in reaching out to celebrities who might be willing to attend.

Several celebrities did attend, including Edward James Olmos; outstanding Dodgers player Steve Garvey; Marilyn McCoo and Billy Davis Jr. of the famous recording group the 5th Dimension; LA Rams star football player and member of the Fearsome Foursome Rosey Grier; and songwriter Al Kasha and his wife, Ceil. It was such a fun night. A line of people stood on the sidewalk. We had photographers, spotlights, a red carpet, a few speeches, and prayer for our city and our church.

We had hoped that this event would get news coverage and create buzz in the media. But our primary goal was to reach more people in our city who might come to visit us just out of curiosity. The publicist we hired had a news company scan the papers and TV for coverage and send us the results. The next day we saw nothing reported. The publicist said it could take a few days. But a few days later, still nothing. It appeared as though no one else cared about our big night. It just didn't seem newsworthy. We were disappointed that we did not get coverage, but our church was inspired and we had created something special. So we moved on.

About two weeks later one of our staff members told me, "The phone is ringing off the hook. Several TV stations and newspapers are looking for a statement or an interview."

"Why?"

"Apparently it went out on the AP newswire that the Hollywood Chamber of Commerce is going to sue us for copyright infringement. They say we created the 'Jesus Star' without their approval."

The chamber of commerce had not contacted us, so this conflict came as a surprise.

"Who wants to talk to us?"

"Everyone. CNN, CBS News, *LA Times, USA Today,* ABC, NBC. It's crazy!"

We set up interviews at the theater to begin about an hour later, and by the time we got there, more news teams had appeared. Television news vans from Telemundo, local KTTV channel 5, Fox, and others were parked around the front of the theater. We had become the hottest story of the day.

News continued throughout the week. Not only did the news coverage span the United States, but it also got exposure in Germany, England, and Japan. Conan O'Brien even mentioned the star in his opening monologue that week. Our church must have gotten about a million dollars' worth of free publicity.

The chamber of commerce did not sue us. I don't think they ever intended to. Throughout the onslaught of calls, questions, and interviews, no legal action had been taken. I think they were frustrated that we didn't check with them first, and their response got blown out of proportion. We apologized for any errors on our part. They were professional and courteous with us. And the publicity was amazing.

Some TV news reporters interviewed random people who walked by the star and asked what they thought. The answers were varied, of course, but my favorite was, "I think that it's interesting that they put a star for Jesus on the sidewalk, but I'll really be impressed when they get His handprints in the cement."

We could not have anticipated that kind of coverage—but God could and did. He took the dream and grew it, in part because we never gave up. We believe Jesus is the star of everything we do, and that is why we gave Him a star in front of our church. But it doesn't end there. We want to help bring Him front and center in the lives of everyone who comes through our doors.

At Oasis Church our goal is to offer a reprieve from the struggles people face as they pursue their dreams. We want to be the place where they receive nourishment, encouragement, and support as they identify their God-dream as well as the guidance they need to stay on track as they move toward it. Whether it is through mentoring, the reassurance they need to persevere, or the faith to let go of burdens and enjoy the journey, we are an oasis on a path that can sometimes feel overwhelming and disheartening.

My prayer and dream for our church has always been to offer the kind of hope and regeneration that an oasis offers to weary travelers, and I believe we have accomplished that in how we serve our community of dreamers. But it all came through perseverance, reaching out to mentors, and being willing to lighten up and be flexible along the way. I hope my example will encourage you to do the same.

|||

**DREAM LOCKS:** Weariness, wanting to quit, and uncertainty in how to improve your work can create discouragement, and feeling lost can put your dream at risk.

**DREAM KEY:** Perseverance allows all other gifts to grow, and unlocking the passion and energy in your heart will help you move forward past the obstacles that threaten your dream.

**SCRIPTURE KEY:** Let us not become weary in doing good, for at the proper time we will reap a harvest if we do not give up. Therefore, as we have opportunity, let us do good to all people, especially to those who belong to the family of believers. (Galatians 6:9–10)

# Dream Thieves

Those who were seen dancing were thought to be
insane by those who could not hear the music.
—ANONYMOUS

The film *Inception* is about a dream within a dream. Leonardo DiCaprio
plays a specialized spy and thief who secretly extracts valuable information
from the unconscious minds of his targets while they dream. When I saw
this movie, I had a dream myself . . . because I fell asleep. So in a sense, I had
a dream within a dream within a dream.

Anyway, DiCaprio's job is to plant the most powerful thing in the world
into people's minds: an idea. He walks into their dreams and places an idea.
That's a powerful notion—invading someone's thoughts with something
that influences their decisions and actions. Those are sacred grounds.

DiCaprio's character brings to mind what I believe is the real reason so
many people struggle to unlock their dreams: dream thieves. Dreams can be
stolen from us because of negative thoughts, disruptive suggestions, or just
distracting ideas that get planted in our brains. These are powerful thieves.

Dream stealers are everywhere: our daily thoughts, past wounds, and
fears of the future. They infiltrate our lives through our friends' comments,
our enemies' accusations, and the mockery of those who don't understand us.
Then we embrace those thoughts and they become self-talk. Essentially we
allow those things that we hear and fear to grow in our minds and become
words that we speak, words that we believe.

The dream thieves we encounter along the way not only can steal our dreams but also can convince us we don't deserve to dream at all. The guilt from mistakes we've made in the past, shame because of judgments made about us, or disqualifying assessments of ourselves become dream thieves. In place of our dreams they leave negative thoughts, discouragement, and continual reruns of our past failures. To unlock the dreams we pursue, we need to recognize these thieves before they break in to our thoughts and pillage all our aspirations.

Dreamers who successfully unlock their dreams know that their paths have been littered with the failed efforts and accusations of would-be thieves. These dreamers are just like people who have not reached their dreams but with one important exception: they don't allow the thieves to steal, kill, or destroy. They push forward in spite of these challenges. That is exactly what you will need to do too.

## Thieves That Are Larger Than Life

Have you ever felt as though you were facing unbelievable odds in pursuing your dream? Those odds then take over your thoughts and make you believe that you can never succeed. If you don't conquer those fears, they only grow bigger. They steal your inspiration by magnifying your obstacles and opposition.

We may want to run from fear, unforgiveness, loneliness, insecurity, and so many other dream thieves, or we may become emotionally or spiritually paralyzed—and so we end up doing nothing. When we allow these thieves to become bigger than they really are, they lock up our dreams tight.

The story of David and Goliath reveals spiritual keys to overcoming the thieves that try to steal the hope that fuels our dreams. Goliath was an undefeated champion warrior. David was a young man—a boy, really—about seventeen years old when he went to the battle lines to take food to his brothers. It was there he faced Goliath when no one else had the courage to try. The unbelievable odds he faced would have been enough to make anyone bolt in the opposite direction. But David had faith in God and decided to fight.

> David said to the Philistine, "You come against me with sword and spear and javelin, but I come against you in the name of the LORD Almighty, the God of the armies of Israel, whom you have defied."[1]

David stood strong and killed Goliath. His thief was a literal giant. Our thieves won't be literal, but they will be mean. They will seem overwhelming. They will come at us from every angle and will be merciless in their pursuit of keeping us from realizing our God-dream. Jesus told us, "The thief comes only to steal and kill and destroy." But He didn't leave us there with no hope. Instead He assured us, "I have come that they may have life, and have it to the full."[2]

> *David put his attention on God, not on Goliath.*
> *I put my attention on Jesus the Healer, not*
> *on cancer; on God, not on my losses.*

In August 2014, I was diagnosed with cancer. I went into treatment for six months. Through that season, I fought not just one thief but what seemed like an entire football team of thieves: weariness, fear, loss, criticism, *and* cancer. When the weariness hit, my mind wanted to fill up with all kinds of scary and negative thoughts. Yet I determined to stand up against the thieves and not let them win my mind, my heart, or my dream. They would not grow into giants.

God was faithful to bring strength and renewal. The cancer is gone now, but my understanding of how thieves work has been redefined. (I will explain more about my cancer battle in another chapter.)

In order to fight thieves, we need to understand how they break into our dreams. By doing that, we discover this truth: what we focus on, we magnify and energize. When we focus on the promises of God, we have no limit to what we can overcome.

I easily could have allowed the thieves of fear and discouragement to steal my dreams and overtake my life, but instead I took my attention off them and put it on God. I could have focused on my diagnosis and how bad I felt from the treatments. I could have allowed the fear that comes with the word *cancer* to overtake me and take my focus off the promises God had for me. Instead I held on to what I knew God was doing in and through me to defeat the thief who was trying to destroy my life and my dreams. David put his attention on God, not on Goliath. I put my attention on Jesus the Healer, not on cancer; on God, not on my losses.

Whether it's our present circumstances or our past, if we are to unlock our dreams, we need to keep our eyes looking forward at where God is leading us.

## Your Past Does Not Hold You Hostage

We all have a past. We all have experiences we wish would never have happened. This thief declares, *Your past disqualifies your dream!* Does your past render you irrevocably limited in your potential? No. It doesn't matter if your past includes things you have done or things that have happened to you; God redeems those things to unlock your God-dreams.

My childhood was framed with dissonance. Because of that, for years my past affected how I dreamed, what I dreamed of, and in many ways, it blocked my ability to hear God's leading. I had to extricate my past from my dreams and allow God to redeem and restore what I'd lost, and I had to use those experiences to build a stronger dream within me.

My dad was an extremely conservative fundamentalist pastor. Growing up I didn't know much about our particular brand of doctrine, but I did know we were against a lot of stuff. What *we* were against, we believed God was against: movies (although television was acceptable), stylish clothing, short dresses, tight pants, long hair (apparently God did not want it to touch either the collar of your shirt or your ears), and rock'n'roll music. (If you had long hair *and* listened to rock'n'roll, that was the 1964 equivalent of devil worship.)

We were against Southern Baptists, Methodists, Pentecostals, and Catholics. We were against women preachers. We looked down on black people— although we would never actually say that. We were definitely against different races marrying each other or even living in the same neighborhoods. I knew more about what we were against than what we were for. It was tough to thrive under this version of Christianity.

It must have been difficult for my mother too. One day when I was eleven years old, while my dad was out of town preaching at a revival meeting, my mother made a decision that blew apart our family's foundation.

"I'm going to leave your dad," she stated. "I can't live like this anymore."

I was the youngest of five children. My oldest brother, Ron, was away at college, and my oldest sister, Sandra, had married and moved away. My brother Tim, my sister Karen, and I still lived with our parents.

Mom continued, "Tim and Karen are going to come with me. You can stay with your dad or you can join us. I would love for you to come with me, but I want you to make the decision." That's a huge choice for an eleven-year-old. No pressure.

When my mom left, my dad had to resign from the church. To fundamentalists, divorce meant your ministry was finished. Dream over.

The problem was that while Dad was dedicated to leading people to faith in Jesus, he was an angry man. Rigid. Broken. Orphaned at seven years old, living in orphanages and on the streets, he never learned how to build relationships. He wasn't a strong leader and couldn't grow with the times. He alienated many people, including his family and friends. And even though he told me he loved me, I never felt the impact of that.

When Mom, Tim, and Karen moved to California, I remained with my dad. I thought maybe if I stayed, it would keep hope alive for eventual restoration.

My hope was briefly renewed a few months later when we all moved to Anaheim, California. But the arguing increased and the intensity escalated. From our living room I could see the famous Disneyland mountain, the Matterhorn. Yet "The Happiest Place on Earth" seemed worlds away. While I watched the nightly fireworks display at Disneyland, I could sense fireworks erupting any moment in our apartment. The police came to our home so often I knew them by name.

"Hi, Officer Turner. Sorry you had to come out here again."

"Parents fighting again?"

"Yes sir." I could only stare at the ground, my eyes wet with tears of fear, embarrassment, and heartbreak.

"Sorry, son. You'll get through this."

The officer was right. It took me about thirty years.

Finally, everyone realized my parents' marriage was really over. When it ended, it wasn't pretty.

While my parents could agree that their marriage was done, they could not agree on which of them would have custody of me. So they fought over custody of me as well as over everything else. I was caught in the middle.

They both kept asking me, "Who would you rather live with?" I felt that if I chose one, I would hurt the other even more than all of this mess already had.

The court decided I needed to appear before the judge in private to let him know which one I wanted to live with. Before the appearance date arrived, I woke up one night to find my dad whispering near my ear, "Tell the judge you want to live with your dad." He repeated this methodically several times, apparently hoping not to awaken me but to plant the thought in my subconscious. #Creepy.

I have a lot of blank spaces in my childhood memories, seasons that have gone missing. That's because during that time, to protect myself, I went inside myself. Deep inside. I was broken and confused with scars on my soul. I was certain that I wasn't worth enough to have dreams of being significant.

Yet during that time God planted a dream in me to help people know the real God. I had a sense that God had something unique for me to do. I just had to figure it out. It took many years of growing, changing, healing, and reinventing to find it. I had to wander through discouragement and conquer despair from my past. I had to silence the thieves that would come and remind me that because of my past, I wasn't worthy of pursuing a God-dream. That I was too broken, too dysfunctional to have the kind of dreams I longed for.

> *I've unlocked my dreams because I've kept my eyes looking forward, not stuck in what was.*

Fast-forward thirty years and I'm the pastor of a church of several thousand people. What's most interesting, however, is that the church is multiracial and practices grace with everybody who enters our doors. How good is God that He took a boy raised in a southern racist city, a prejudiced church, and a bigoted family, and changed me so much that I embraced a God-dream that includes ministering to *all* people. Today Oasis Church is one of the most racially diverse churches that many people have ever experienced. It has become a key component of my and my church's God-dream. Racial diversity was not our goal. It just happened, and we realized how special it was, so we have tried to nurture it and protect this gift from God.

Today, it is the number one question leaders ask me: How did you do it? How can we do that at our church? I believe many people are racist in some way but don't realize it. When we put up a barrier against a certain type of people, that locks up and hinders our ability to truly realize our dreams, as we'll talk more about in chapter 13.

It took time for me to see my God-dream, to embrace it, and it continues to take time to come to fruition. Today I've unlocked my dreams because I've kept my eyes looking forward, not stuck in what was—and not listening to the dream thieves that get in my mind and accuse me.

Your past doesn't have to hold you hostage. If you trust God and follow Him, He will redeem and restore—and even use!—your past. Harmony Dust Grillo knows this intimately, and her story is a great example for us as we unlock our dreams.

When Harmony was a young girl, her father abandoned her, and she saw him only a dozen times throughout her childhood.

As she grew older, she was sexually abused by several people, both men and women. The abuse left her covered in shame, and she began to believe that something must be inherently wrong with her since she kept attracting that kind of attention. Her self-esteem was so wounded that later when she found a boyfriend, she became a slave to his manipulations and sacrificed her dignity to stay with him.

After high school, a friend suggested she could earn "great money" as a stripper. She agreed, thinking she would work there only two or three months. She stayed for three years.

One day, Harmony befriended a girl in a ballet class she was taking. This girl was a Christian who invited her to Oasis Church. Eventually Harmony agreed because she felt the girl was genuine; the girl had never made her friendship contingent on Harmony quitting stripping or going to church. The first time Harmony walked into our church building, she felt as if she'd come home. So she kept returning. After she had spent about six months attending services, God began to bring healing to her heart. It became hard for Harmony to live the life of a stripper and grow in her new freedom.

"I began attending [Oasis] Church, and like a gentleman, God pursued me with his infinite love until he captured my heart," Harmony explains. "Hearing the pastor talk about the idea that I was created with a purpose stirred something in me. I remember the night that I was standing in the middle of the strip club and it really hit me: *I have been created with a purpose.*"

As she looked around the strip club, she realized, *This can't be it.* God was planting a dream in her. "I discovered that the pain of staying the same is far greater than the pain of change," Harmony says. Soon she quit dancing, left the abusive boyfriend, and began a journey of walking with God and allowing Him to heal her. Harmony admits, "It hasn't always been easy, but God is good and has been with me every step of the way." God showed her, she says, "my beauty and worth—to help me see the value I never saw in myself."[3]

Harmony went on to pursue a master's in social welfare, and in 2003, she founded Treasures Ministries.[4] Now Harmony ministers to women in the sex industry through gift bags, prayer support, and counseling. She has trained outreach leaders who have gone on to establish more than one hundred sex-industry outreaches on five continents. She has been featured in *Glamour* magazine, on the *Dr. Drew* show, and on *The Tyra Banks Show,* among other media outlets. She's even written her memoir, *Scars and Stilettos,* in which she gives an account of the journey she took "from working in strip clubs, to leading an organization that reaches women in the sex industry.

"These women are completely taken aback [by the love we show as we reach out to them], which shows me that my outreach needs to be about loving them for the sake of loving them," Harmony says. "It's not our responsibility to convict women to stop stripping—that's the Holy Spirit's job. Instead, we just let them know that there is a God who loves them beyond their wildest dreams."[5]

Harmony refused to allow her past to steal what God had planted in her heart and mind. She would not let the thieves of criticism, discouragement, negative thoughts, or past failures limit her future but used them as a catalyst to make a difference in the world.

## Three Keys to Stop Thieves from Stealing Your Dream

We can't just wish away thieves. We must be proactive. I've found these three keys can stop dream thieves in their tracks.

### Key 1: Practice Gratitude

When thieves prowl into our minds and threaten our dreams, we have a choice in how we respond. One response is to wallow in the dark side, which leads us to become ungrateful for the dream God has created specifically for us. Ungratefulness is a powerful opponent that steals our focus, and without a bold response to reverse our attitude, ultimately it can sabotage our dreams. Ingratitude is one of the most destructive ways to respond to dream thieves. It may feel like a normal response to pain and disappointment, but it usually makes things harder than they need to be.

Turning our attitude from frustrated to grateful changes our perspective. It opens the heavens and makes us aware that God is actually giving us gifts every day—and that those gifts offer numerous opportunities to unlock our dreams.

I've learned to practice thankfulness. I began to express my gratitude for things that seem amazing and even for the things that seem insignificant.

That's a great starting place, and as we practice being thankful for the small things, our minds begin to open us to gratitude for the harder things.

If you are unsure of what to do in your situation right now and your dream seems to be in permanent lockdown, know that the will of God for you always includes gratitude. As the apostle Paul said, "Give thanks in all circumstances; for this is God's will for you in Christ Jesus."[6]

*In all circumstances*—in everything I will be thankful. That's a powerful key.

I keep a dream notebook for writing down the dreams I have and the hopes, fears, promises, obstacles, and realizations that come in the process. When I feel myself slipping into ungratefulness, the list making in my dream notebook begins. It looks something like this:

I'm thankful for
- the lunch today with friends, the book I read yesterday, the movie I saw last week
- my home, my family, my church
- peace, strength, rest for the battles I'm facing

When the thieves show up in our minds to steal our dreams, we need to be armed with gratitude.

*I expected better circumstances. I expected kinder people.*

Standing behind these thoughts is the thief I call ungratefulness and the stealth-like destructive work of our own expectations.

*This is not what I thought would happen. That's why I'm disappointed. That's why I'm dissatisfied.*

When we entertain these thoughts, we become even more ungrateful and the cycle continues. Ingratitude dulls and sours our vision. When what we have right now seems as if it's not enough, our heart disengages from the power of faith and attaches its focus to disappointment and despair.

*I did not expect this loss. I did not expect this disappointment or this pain.*

But our enemy did not expect that somewhere inside us a whisper can arise: *"I will yet praise him."*[7] Even though I thought this would be easier, I will praise Him because He hasn't given up on me.

The whisper becomes a shout as we recognize the power in it.

*Even though I've had this setback, yet I will praise God and thank Him for what He has done and is doing—even when I can't see His work right now.*

When we start to thank God, our faith moves from a trickle of water to the strength of a forceful river. When we become more aware of His gifts to us and we give thanks for them, we experience joy, and strength emerges. Reality is clearer. I suspect that the unhappiest dreamers are the most ungrateful, a risk you and I can't afford to take. Gratitude is a much better option.

### Key 2: Keep the Faith

People and heartbreaks go together way too often. People and joy go together also. How do we handle the heartbreaks? This is a life and death question. The part of our hearts that loves life and loves people is the same part that screams when broken. The part of our hearts that dreams big dreams and pursues imaginative goals is the part that we have to take care of and nurture when our hearts have been shattered.

What breaks our hearts? Loss. Separation, abandonment, death, transitions, lies, hidden agendas, and a myriad of other potential dream crushers. We can't let them keep us from believing deeply that we were created to have and pursue dreams, from believing that God has placed specific dreams within us that work out of our specific talents. In the midst of heartbreak, grasping on to faith helps us find a place after loss and grief where we can say, "It is well with my soul." Where we can retrieve our dreams from this thief's hands.

I drove with a friend one afternoon to hear a guest speaker at a church. My energy was low and my faith wavering from a recent disappointment. It was a rainy day, and my brain was telling me what my heart struggled to believe: *Everything will be okay.*

The speaker told a familiar story that I'd heard before, but it still inspired me, because I needed to find a faith greater than my circumstances. The story was about Horatio Spafford, a wealthy and thriving Chicago lawyer who owned a beautiful home and had a loving wife and family. He was also a dedicated Christian.

At the peak of his success, however, he suffered a great loss when his only son died. And then another tragedy hit when the Great Chicago Fire destroyed almost every real-estate investment he had. Later, he planned a trip to Europe with his family. Some last-minute business arose, so he sent his wife and four daughters ahead, with the intent to follow them once he handled his affairs. But tragedy struck again when he received word that the ship his family had been on sank, killing more than two hundred people on board, including all of his daughters. He received a telegram from his wife, which stated, "Alone survived. What shall I do?"

Spafford boarded a ship right away that would take him to his wife in England. He was heartbroken and in anguish. As his ship passed the area where his daughters had drowned, he penned the words that would become a reminder to millions of Christians of what unshakable faith really is.

When sorrows like sea billows roll,
Whatever my lot, Thou hast taught me to say,
"It is well, it is well with my soul."[8]

Horatio Spafford had great successes, but clearly he was not unfamiliar with pain, tears, and tragedy. Yet his faith seems to come from somewhere unfamiliar to many dreamers. He was ruled by a faith that was bigger than the circumstances he endured. In the face of heartbreaking experiences, you and I must cling to that kind of faith, a faith that allows our ability to dream to remain intact.

Our faith grows strong against the thieves of heartbreak when we live in the reality of Paul's revelation: "The peace of God, which surpasses all understanding, will guard your hearts and minds through Christ Jesus."[9]

### Key 3: Keep Your Passion Alive

Limitations are everywhere and can feel relentless. As we pursue our dreams, we ask ourselves, *Is this a fantasy I'm trying to make a reality, or is it actually possible? If it is possible, do I have what it takes? Am I good enough? Will I fail? Am I a valuable person without any accomplishments? If people look closely enough, will they see that I am not enough?* These are the questions that insecurity poses to us.

A dream stealer enters our pursuits when what is actually possible is camouflaged among the real impossibilities we encounter. When we see what looks to be impossible, we often not only begin to doubt the possibilities, but we also begin to doubt our ability. One feeds the other. We become uncertain of our value or significance. What is possible looks impossible when the accompanying gangsters of inadequacy, insignificance, and insufficiency are allowed into the story. But impossible is not a fact. It's an opinion. And we must cling to our focused passion to keep this thief from stealing our dreams.

George Dantzig understood that kind of passion. While enrolled in the mathematics doctoral program at the University of California, Berkeley, he arrived late to one of his classes. He saw two statistical problems written on the blackboard and assumed them to be a homework assignment.

He went home and worked to solve both. When he turned in the assignment late, he apologized to his professor, saying that "the problems seemed harder to do than usual." What Dantzig hadn't realized was that both of the statistical problems on the board had been two famous unsolved problems.[10] But Dantzig did not know the problems were unsolvable, so he solved them. He went on to become a mathematical scientist and professor who won many awards for his work. I believe it was his passion that allowed him not to give up.

He didn't know he wasn't supposed to be able to solve those problems. Had he come to class on time and heard that assessment, would he have tried to solve them? I don't know. I would hope that even hearing his professor's claim, he would have still at least tried. That's what God calls us to do.

After a few months of being in ministry, I realized that hidden inside me was the desire to be a successful pastor so people would respect me. That desire was alarmingly larger than the desire to help people and, for a while, caused me to become unrealistically focused on any criticism that people expressed. We cannot be passionate or fully effective in unlocking our dreams if we worry about what everybody thinks. We must passionately cling to the conviction that the truth matters more than what someone thinks of us or our dreams.

We always need to recognize, reject, and overcome those thieves that try to make our self-talk negative. Dreamers who reach their goal do it because they've locked up thieves who have tried to make them victims. You and I are not victims! God didn't make any mistakes when He planted those dreams within us. Now let's lock the thieves out of our minds and unlock our true potential.

|||

**DREAM LOCKS:** Negative thoughts, discouragement, and relentless opposition can become thieves who steal your dreams, maybe even robbing you of the capacity to dream.

**DREAM KEY:** Keep dream thieves out of your treasured journey by practicing gratitude, faith, passion, and a forward outlook.

**SCRIPTURE KEY:** In all these things we are more than conquerors through him who loved us. For I am convinced that neither death nor life, neither angels nor demons, neither the present nor the future, nor any powers, neither height nor depth, nor anything else in all creation, will be able to separate us from the love of God that is in Christ Jesus our Lord. (Romans 8:37–39)

# Choosing Friends

[Friends] cherish each other's hopes. They are kind to
each other's dreams.

—Henry David Thoreau,
*A Week on the Concord and Merrimack Rivers*

Holly and I have gone scuba diving in some of the great locations in the world. Once we went on a "feed the sharks" dive off the coast of Florida. It involved diving down fifty feet with an instructor who gathered all the divers in a circle on the ocean floor. He sat in the middle and pulled out fish from a container. Soon nurse sharks came around us, and while he fed them, we watched the sharks up close. Nurse sharks are not aggressive; they have small mouths and small teeth. These are important facts.

It wasn't until we were sitting on the ocean bottom surrounded by fifteen hungry sharks that I asked myself what now seemed like vital questions that should have come up *before* I jumped in the middle of a bunch of sharks.

*How does the instructor know that all of these guys are nurse sharks? I can't tell the difference between nurse sharks and the tourist-eating sharks.*

*Do these sharks understand the agreement we have about only eating the little fishies we are feeding them and not the little fingers we are holding the bait with?*

*Have there been any "feed the sharks" dives that went terribly wrong?*

I realized we had put a lot of trust in our dive guide. We put a lot of trust in the sharks too. They seemed really hungry. They were doing what they do best: aggressively eating fish. I was hoping not to make an unplanned appearance on *Shark Week*. This expression of trust worked out well because they all behaved and we emerged from the ocean with all our fingers and other important extremities intact.

There's another level of trust we need to experience if we're going to unlock our dreams: we have to trust the friends in our lives.

Trust is crucial for friendships, and it is essential to learn how to trust little by little rather than enthusiastically doing away with that part of the friendship-building process. I'm talking about trusting people with small matters and slowly increasing trust as they show you how they treat what you have trusted them with—rather than going all in immediately. Small steps is a wiser approach. We have to be confident in what and in whom we put our trust.

A good way to start is by asking yourself some simple questions. Do they respect what you respect? Do they support what's important to you, or do they criticize it?

One example of trusting gradually is how I advise single moms who begin dating someone new. I recommend they give their friend time to earn the opportunity to meet their children, that they resist the urge to introduce them right away. Our children are so important, and just as a parent would vet baby-sitters or nannies before hiring them, single mothers need time to know for sure that they have a future with the person they are dating and that the guy is trustworthy enough to let him into that part of their lives. Moms who don't take this precaution often regret it later.

Friendships can make or break you *and* your dreams. There is nothing like a friend's support, and building relationships with people who have different strengths will create a great circle of strength in your life. As Walt Disney said, "You can design and create, and build the most wonderful place in the world. But it takes people to make the dream a reality."[1]

Having someone who knows you—your strengths, your weaknesses, your successes, and your failures—and still stands by you is a comfort that cannot be replaced. But allowing someone into your inner circle of trust who isn't supportive or doesn't have your best interests at heart can derail you from achieving your dreams. Whether a person discourages and criticizes your dreams, tries to convince you not to pursue them, or envies your success, having someone work against you can be worse than just not having support.

Having a friend beside me as I pursue my dreams has made all the difference. I have friends who talk to me, confide in me, and listen to me when I tell them my concerns. Even when I have been knocked down because of something a friend has said or done, it's still the strength of another friend that has helped me get back up and press on.

One of the most challenging of all life skills is the ability to choose the right people to help us unlock our dreams. We will not reach our dreams alone. We need others we can trust who will help us, who will be honest with us, and who will encourage and challenge us. The dreams God gives us are often crafted in a way that causes us to need the help of others in order to fulfill them. God is tricky that way. *You know that dream I gave you, the one you keep thinking about?* He whispers. *It's going to take building friendships. In fact, if you can't build the right friendships, you are not going to make it.*

### Build a Dream Team

I like the idea of having a dream team. Developing one could be the best project we ever invest in for reaching our dreams. A dream team is an unofficial group of supporters we can rely on and trust, each with different gifts or strengths. An old African proverb says, "If you want to go fast, go alone. If you want to go far, go together."

These team members don't just appear, however; we have to find them and recruit them. And perhaps hardest of all, we have to love them and allow them to love us back (because they aren't just in our lives for us to *use*). For some people this comes naturally, and for others it takes work.

Your dream team could include, among others, someone who is wise in business, one who is a good communicator, another who has strong faith, and one who is a great encourager. It wouldn't hurt if one of them could dunk a basketball, but that's not actually necessary unless you are building a basketball dream team.

Social media has helped create or perpetuate a false sense of relationships. Friendships are not the same as *followers* on Twitter. We can't equate our friendships with Likes on Instagram. We settle for substitutes for real relationships and end up lacking the kind of friends who bring their lives alongside ours.

A good friend has that unusual ability to encourage you, stand with you, and still be able to tell you when you are being ridiculous. You actually need that friend who will tell you if something green is stuck between your teeth.

If they aren't willing to be honest when it's something simple like a poor fashion choice, how helpful will they be when it really matters, when it involves your dream? Will they encourage you to audition for *The Voice* when you can't carry a tune? Will they say something when you announce you plan to try out for the basketball team, even though you have only about a six-inch vertical jump? If your dream isn't realistic, good friends not only will let you know it's not a good idea to pursue; they will help you identify where your gifts are.

I've heard people say, "If at the end of your life, you have three or four really good friends, you are a lucky person." That seems like it's aiming low. Why only three? Shouldn't we have a lot more? Wouldn't more friends help us be better in our pursuits?

Now that I've lived a few decades, I get the "three or four friends" idea. I have often misread a person and the signals he gives about his values and integrity. I've trusted the wrong people while keeping the right ones at arm's length. I've not invested time in the right people. I've invested a lot of heart into people who have moved on geographically or metaphorically and not enough in those who will be with me longer.

If you want to unlock your dream, then you need to build a dream team who can call you out when you are on the wrong track, cheer for you as you struggle along the right one, and lift you when you fall. How do you make new friends you can trust? How do you broaden your relationship circle?

Let's look at some key characteristics these dream-team friends need to have.

### The Friend Who Makes You a Better Person

On your friendship dream team you need someone who brings strength to your life, someone who is willing to encourage—and challenge—you. If you surround yourself only with people who agree with you, then you will never fully unlock your potential or your dreams. Instead you need at least one friend who will point out your inconsistencies and push you to be better. This person won't always be your favorite, but having someone on your team who is willing to be honest and confront you on your *issues* can be a lifesaver. If you are willing to keep people like this around, they will compel you to grow, to be honest, and to be aware of your attitude.

"Genuine friendship cannot possibly exist where one of the parties is unwilling to hear truth and the other is equally indisposed to speak it," said Roman philosopher Cicero. We need the type of "tell it like it is" friend who won't be satisfied with our stagnant status quo. That input can be difficult to hear, but as King Solomon said, "As iron sharpens iron, so a friend sharpens a friend."[2]

We need this person to offer constructive criticism, which we then need to accept. We need someone to call us out when we are being self-absorbed, whiny, pessimistic, foolish, arrogant, or any of the other things we tend to be when we are focused only on what *we* want. This is essential to staying on the right path to our God-dreams.

You probably have people in your life right now who fit this category, but maybe you've never considered making a closer connection with them. Reach out, take the chance, and let them be friends to you.

### The Friend Who Inspires You to Keep Going

The next friend on your dream team needs to be someone who draws strength out of you so that you are able to do what seemed too difficult before. Several years ago Admiral William H. McRaven gave a speech to the graduates of the University of Texas at Austin in which he talked about an aspect of the Navy SEALs training called Hell Week.

This one week in particular is the roughest, toughest part. It consists of no sleep, constant calisthenics, long runs, and relentless mental and physical harassment.

By the end of the week, the sailors must pass one last brutal test. There is an area between San Diego and Tijuana known as the Tijuana Sloughs, which is a swampy, muddy pit that can swallow you up. The sailors spend fifteen hours in that mud up to their necks, trying to survive the freezing cold and winds. As they're in this environment, the instructors add pressure to quit by taunting them mercilessly.

Admiral McRaven shared about his own experience in the mud flats.

As the sun began to set that Wednesday evening, my training class, having committed some "egregious infraction of the rules" was ordered into the mud.

The mud consumed each man till there was nothing visible but our heads. The instructors told us we could leave the mud if only five men would quit—just five men—and we could get out of the oppressive cold. Looking around the mud flat it was apparent that some students were about to give up. It was still over eight hours till the sun came up—eight more hours of bone-chilling cold.

The chattering teeth and shivering moans of the trainees were so loud it was hard to hear anything. And then, one voice began to echo through the night, one voice raised in song. The song was terribly out of tune, but sung with great enthusiasm. One voice became two and two became three and before long everyone in the class was singing. We knew that if one man could rise above the misery then others could as well.

The instructors threatened us with more time in the mud if we kept up the singing, but the singing persisted. And somehow the mud seemed a little warmer, the wind a little tamer and the dawn not so far away.[3]

There is great power in being surrounded by friends who can help you declare your faith in the darkest hours. It can bring hope and perseverance, and even more powerfully, it can bring the presence of God. As Jesus reminds us, "Where two or three gather in my name, there am I with them."[4]

Friends who bring this stabilizing element inspire us to live on a higher level. They stir within us a deep desire to be better because we see how they live, and that modeling challenges us to keep reaching for our dreams. When we hang around these friends we get stronger. We pick up their attitudes. The vision for what could be grows, we discover a greater sense of self-respect, and we become more willing to risk. We can go on even when everything within us doubts or wants to quit.

### The Friend You Marry

I suppose I'm a bit of a romantic. I'm not suggesting that my wife would say, "Wow! Philip is so romantic." I mean that I have romantic ideas about life, love, dreams, and people. As far as my marriage goes, though, I randomly think of romantic ideas and try to apply them. I have bursts of romantic genius that make me think I've made a major deposit in the romance bank and that I should be able to coast for a while.

One marriage notion that isn't just romantic but *essential* is that your spouse helps you unlock your dreams rather than blocks them. One of my greatest gifts was that Holly was totally on board with my dream to start Oasis Church. Even during those early years when the money was tight and I wondered if my dream would ever succeed, she stayed committed to it and encouraged me.

Having a spouse who encourages your dreams doesn't mean marriage is supposed to be easy, though. Holly and I have a high-maintenance marriage. It takes work. The work couples do in marriage, though, is not supposed to be a prison sentence of "life with hard labor." The work part is so you can have the enjoyable part. Some couples never find that part. All work and no play ruins a marriage—and dreams. You don't have to do something awful to destroy your marriage; you just have to do *nothing*. When all your attention is on handling conflicts, you can easily forget the friendship part. But keeping the friendship factor as a core aspect of your relationship carries you through challenges to your life, marriage, and dreams.

Even after thirty years of marriage, Holly and I can still get sidetracked into debates or maneuvering to get our way so that we forget to protect and nurture our friendship. This scene played out not too long ago:

"I don't understand why we need all these pillows on the bed," I said, not realizing where that comment would lead us.

"It looks better with them. You need to trust me on this. It's a woman thing," she explained.

"Are a vast number of pillows decorating the bed actually a *thing*?"

"Yes. It's a *thing*," she assured me.

"Would just four or five still look good, or do we need all twenty-three pillows?"

"You always claim that I exaggerate, but you're the one exaggerating now."

"I don't *always* say that you do. Just sometimes. I just think it's funny."

"Count the pillows," she said, with a slight edge.

"That's not the point. I *am* exaggerating. But I'm just playing with you."

*"Count the pillows."*

"One, two, three . . . nine. There are nine pillows on our bed. Not one that says anything masculine, by the way. If we could put an LA Dodgers pillow on there, that would make it an even ten, and I could relate a little more to your pillow strategy."

"That's not going to happen. I want our room to look nice when people come to visit. Bedroom décor is not your strong suit."

"Who comes over that we need to give them a tour of our bedroom?" I wondered out loud, not ready to surrender.

"Just leave it alone, okay? Let's talk about something else."

"Well, show me one more time how you want them."

"I've shown you a thousand times." (As in one thousand equals about five! Or maybe twelve.)

"I love you so much. Isn't this great? I love these moments. I want to remember us the way we are right now," I said, trying to lighten the mood that I'd helped create. It didn't work. "Okay, no problem. You're right. It looks great. Really." I smiled. "We can keep the pillows just how you set them up. All nine! Let me take a picture with my phone so I can remember how you have them because you never know when the president of the United States might drop by."

*This* is what I mean by high maintenance. And now you know why we need prayer. Perhaps this is why Benjamin Franklin stated, "Keep your eyes wide open before marriage, half shut afterwards." But there is no friend more important than your spouse, especially when it comes to reaching your dreams.

I'm in love with Holly. After you pass the thirty-year mark, it's official. I'm in love with my wife. I love her smile. I love her hair. I love her laugh. I love how she has never met a stranger. I love how she usually spills whatever she's eating on her blouse, even in expensive restaurants.

Holly tells me that I write about my feelings better than I talk about them. She has this opinion because when I write a love note or fill in the blank spaces on a birthday or anniversary card, she often says something like, "I love what you wrote here. I wish you spoke like you write. But I'll take the notes."

Holly loves romance. She loves to be shown that she is valuable (as all spouses do). I don't always get it right. I think the basic theory of effective romance is that a lifestyle of ongoing small romantic gestures is better than a one-time romantic "big event." If you never show any romantic efforts until the anniversary comes around each year, your big efforts won't have the same impact as the big effort surrounded by a lot of smaller efforts. That too is about maintaining your marriage friendship.

If you are married, it's probably time to invest some romance into that relationship you've always dreamed of, or else it could become the nightmare you always wanted to avoid.

## The Friend We Have to Walk Away From

Friendships are built around agreements, shared values, and connection. But some friendships will hinder our ability to pursue our dreams. The hardest thing is to walk away when a relationship gets too toxic. I'm not talking about the typical disagreement or frustration that occurs in all relationships. If we walk away from friendships with those who challenge us to be better, our relationships can't grow, so I'm not talking about that kind of disagreement or frustration. I'm talking about the friendships that really destroy who God has called us to be.

People who are close to us can be a determining factor in our ability to reach our dreams, but they can sabotage those dreams as well. A friendship that becomes toxic and is seasoned with criticism and negativity drains our physical energy and our emotions.

> *It takes only one Jonah on your boat*
> *to bring more storms into your life.*

Whether we realize that the friendship has relied on unhealthy expectations we no longer can maintain or we become aware that we are heading in different directions, there comes a moment when we have to walk away from all the drama and the people who create it. This is a difficult decision, but it is vital.

Conflict arises when we are growing in an aspect of our character that one of our friends is not also growing in. Some friends may not like to see us moving forward and doing bigger things, so they speak negativity and discouragement into our lives. They try to derail our progress, whether unconsciously or overtly, because they are dissatisfied with their own position. Maybe they haven't discovered their own God-dream, or maybe they have veered off the path. Either way, they do not contribute positively to our journey and it becomes necessary to distance ourselves from them.

Sometimes our values aren't the same as our friends' anymore. Some friends do not treat us with honor. Some relationships become more and more critical, dishonest, or abusive, and we have to walk away. These friends will never help us unlock our dream's potential.

There are also those friends who will make life choices that are huge violations of your values. You can still love them but may not be able to continue to do life with them in the same capacity. These are friends who will hinder your dreams.

Friends who once were supportive but who have become negative forces can be dead weight that holds you back. Maybe this is a season of your life when it is necessary to rely on others. You can be sentimental or you can free yourself to move forward. You should not have friends like these on your dream team, nor should you entertain their expectations for your dreams.

When the Old Testament prophet Jonah ran away from God's call on his life, he "escaped" on a ship. Soon the ship hit a big storm. The boat's and crew's safety were in danger. Jonah realized that God was trying to stop him from running away. " 'Pick me up and throw me into the sea,' he replied, 'and it will become calm. I know that it is my fault that this great storm has come upon you.' "[5] When they did throw him overboard, the sea became calm.

We can learn an important lesson from Jonah's story. I'm not saying you should literally throw someone overboard, but if someone in your life is sinking your ship, it is time to put distance between you and that person. It takes only one Jonah on your boat to bring more storms into your life. Surround yourself with people who make you laugh, forget the bad, and focus on the good. Love the people who treat you right. Pray for the ones who don't. Life is too short to be in broken relationships.

## The Friends Who Need You to Help Them Reach Their Dreams

There's one more kind of friend you need on your dream team. These are the friends who need *you* to help them unlock *their* dreams.

On a trip to Uganda, I visited a small community called Peche Village, near Gulu. Our charity, Generosity.org, had built a hand-pump water well there. As our group stood and talked about the excitement of this new well, a young boy came up to me. He looked me in the eye and asked, "Will you be my friend?" His simple and sincere question surprised me.

"Of course I'll be your friend," I said, hoping I was doing the right thing. "My name is Philip. What's yours?"

"Daniel," he replied.

I asked one of our hosts, "If a boy in this village asks me to be his friend, does he want something specific from me?" I wasn't sure what I wasn't sure about. "When I said yes, does he expect something from me? I'm not sure what I've said yes to."

"I think he just wants to know that someone beyond his village cares about him," our guide assured me.

I invited an interpreter over so I could be sure I communicated and understood everything correctly. Then I asked Daniel about himself and what he liked to do. I hoped to find some common ground.

> *When the planes hit the Twin Towers, as far as I know, none of the phone calls from the people on board were messages of hate or revenge—they were all messages of love. If you look for it, I've got a sneaky feeling you'll find that love actually is all around.*
> —The Prime Minister, *Love Actually*

"Do you go to school?"

"I used to go, but I got kicked out," he said, turning away with a look of embarrassment.

"Kicked out? Why?"

"We don't have money to pay the fees."

As soon as I heard his answer, my suspicions were aroused once again. It's interesting how suspicion creeps into our minds when someone needs help. *Are they going to take advantage of me?* we wonder. Kind of like when someone approaches us at the gas station and says, "Can you help me out with a dollar or two so I can get gas? My family is in the car down the street waiting for me. It's really important. Please?" Don't these guys know that thousands of people try this at gas stations all over the country?

I took a deep breath and decided to see where the conversation went. "Oh," I told Daniel. "How much are your school fees?" I imagined the fees would cost several hundred dollars.

The interpreter quizzed Daniel for a minute and then told me, "It's about forty-five dollars a year. He's missed the last two months."

"A whole year? Forty-five dollars? He had to stop because of two months? I can pay for this," I said, feeling a little like Bill Gates at his philanthropic best. This young boy, who was now my friend, was not going to miss out on school because of a measly forty-five dollars. So I arranged with the local school to pay his school fees. That was seven years ago. I'm still sponsoring him.

His full name is Komakech Daniel. *Komakech* means "I am unfortunate" or "cursed." There is a kind of beauty naming a child the African way, as African people attach meanings to names based on situations and circumstances, and sometimes the dreams they have for their lives. This tradition was carried on within the LRA (Lord's Resistance Army) camps with mothers choosing meaningful names for their offspring. But the majority of abducted mothers gave their children names reflecting their plight and thus referring to their abduction, servitude, sexual slavery, and their endless desire to return home.[6]

Many children in Uganda are named Komakech. Imagine thousands of children throughout Uganda being called day after day, "Cursed one, unfortunate one, come home to eat."

A pastor I know, Chris Komagum, was born Komakech Chris, but he changed his name to Komagum ("I am fortunate") because of his faith. He realized that his faith in Jesus changed him. He is not unfortunate; he is blessed.

My young friend Daniel now attends school and is growing in confidence, faith, and vision for his life. Each year when I go back and see him, he has gotten bigger, and I remember that day we started our friendship. My yes to him grew out of my own dream to help others. But it did something more: it offered him an opportunity to unlock his dreams as well. That's what friends are for, to lend each other a hand, right?

As we pursue our dreams, it is important to first know we have embraced our God-dream. Once we are on that path, we will encounter different types of dream thieves, so it is vital that we surround ourselves with healthy relationships to support us in that journey. We also have to make sure we eliminate, or at the very least minimize, the impact of those who are not helping us along the way. The friends we choose to have in our lives can determine how well our dreams come together and how we manage them once we are there. Find your dream team and allow them to help you unlock your dreams.

|||

**DREAM LOCKS:** Isolation, loneliness, and independence can be destructive to your dream, causing you to struggle more than you need to in your pursuits.

**DREAM KEY:** Invest in friends you can trust who will believe in you, encourage you, challenge you, and inspire you. Walk away from those friends who have their own expectations for what dream you should have or who discourage or demoralize you.

**SCRIPTURE KEY:** One who has unreliable friends soon comes to ruin, but there is a friend who sticks closer than a brother. (Proverbs 18:24)

# The Unwelcome Crisis

There cannot be a crisis next week. My schedule is already full

—HENRY KISSINGER

It started like a normal day at the beach, only the tide was extremely low. Tourists were out enjoying their reprieve from the stresses of their everyday lives back home, unaware of the incoming tsunami. Some vacationers played in the water, while others wandered about enjoying time in the sun.

Soon people noticed giant waves on the horizon. As the waves got closer, they also noticed that the boats were trying to escape the waves. When the first wave reached one ship and swallowed it whole, the tourists on the beach recognized the magnitude of what was coming directly at them. Within moments people were dragged under the fierce waters of the Indian Ocean tsunami of Boxing Day 2004.

Moments before paradise was smashed into a million pieces, a mother relaxed on a lounge chair while her family played nearby on the beach with their dad. As this phenomenon unfolded and waves rushed in, she watched in horror as her husband and their two youngest boys disappeared under the mass of water that carried with it cars and the chalet the family had been staying in.

The tragedy struck seemingly out of nowhere. It was a literal example of what people feel in the face of life's crises—cancer, death, loss of a thousand different kinds. One minute things are great. We are laughing and playing, and the next moment we are hit with a storm. We are left with a myriad of questions: *How do I survive this? Will my life ever be normal again? How do I pursue my dreams in the middle of this pain?*

I was one of those people. The note in my journal for August 15, 2014, reads:

*I found out today I have cancer.*

That was the entire entry. It summed things up pretty well. I didn't know what else to write.

I was in Charmhaven, Australia, with my wife. We were speaking at a relationship conference at Hope Unlimited Church, where Mark and Darlene Zschech pastor. Holly and I were eating breakfast in our hotel when my doctor called. I had recently had a comprehensive physical, along with a biopsy on a lump that had appeared on my scalp.

"The biopsy test was positive for cancer. It's a lymphoma," the doctor said. I found it difficult to focus as she continued to explain more. But I did hear her say, "It's a less aggressive kind. I'm really sorry I have to tell you this over the phone, but I wanted you to know as soon as we found out."

As the news sunk in, I thought, *I'm supposed to speak tonight. How am I going to do that?* Holly could see on my face that there was a problem.

"You will have to meet with an oncologist who can do more tests, determine the type of lymphoma, and recommend treatment."

Fear punched me in the gut. My thoughts weren't clear, and I felt a series of diverse emotions and thoughts rush through me. *What does this mean? What am I supposed to do next? Am I going to be okay? Can we beat this? I don't think I can do this. I think . . . I think . . . I don't know what to think. I believe Jesus is my Healer.*

When you hear the word *cancer* spoken about you, it brings with it a thousand wearisome thoughts. The doctor said it wasn't the most aggressive type and was only in that one location on my scalp, but it was a type of cancer in the blood, so it could exist in other places in my body, though undetectable at that point.

We remembered the situation ten years earlier when Holly and I were in the doctor's office and heard the diagnosis of her breast cancer. The conversations, the emotions, and the journey that I'd rather not have been on came vividly to mind. I remembered how our lives went through tremendous chaos, change, and emotional ups and downs. I thought of all we'd learned about cancer, faith, nutrition, physical and emotional health, community, and more.

*Here we go again.*

I'd already been battling fatigue for about a year. Now my energy level crashed through the floor.

The feeling that, for the moment, I could not tell anyone about what I was facing felt overwhelming. We had dinners, met with people, did ministry, prayed, and worshiped while our hearts held on to what we were now dealing with. Surreal.

Once we told our kids, our friends, and our church, the pressure of keeping things quiet lifted. Then my battle became about staying focused.

Crisis comes to visit all of us. Maybe a bad habit or a bad decision finds us at the bottom of a pit. Or maybe a cloud of crisis has cast a dark shadow on our future. It is the unwelcome visitor. It usually brings an entourage with it. They are not our friends, but we recognize them: fear, discouragement, anger, and so many others. All of these "guests" come home with us, uninvited, and sit at the table for dinner. Then they stay. They sit by us while we watch TV, or they whisper to us when we take a shower. #Relentless.

We know that a crisis will come. Learning to turn it into victory becomes more than a cliché in the middle of the battle. It's a mission statement: this crisis will not crush dreams!

We have to believe that our dreams are still intact and that we have a God-designed purpose, that we can use the crisis to keep ourselves focused and committed to what God has planned for us.

## Pursuing a God-Dream Doesn't
## Guarantee a Crisis-Free Life

Often we can fall into the belief that because God gave us a dream to pursue, we are somehow protected from the trials and troubles that Jesus said would fall on everyone.[1] As I went through my battle against cancer, I became aware of the hidden belief that I had stored away in my subconscious: *The stronger my faith, the fewer problems will come my way.* Man, was that wrong!

When I received my diagnosis, I was already in the middle of one of the most challenging years for my life, ministry, and dreams. Now I had to throw cancer into the mix.

In 2013 our church had celebrated fulfilling one of the most exciting dreams of our thirty years: buying the amazing church building I talked about in chapter 5. Our membership grew by a thousand people in just a couple of weeks after we moved in. It was like four consecutive Easter Sundays. People were everywhere! They were making decisions to follow Jesus and experiencing dynamic life change. My dreams were becoming a reality!

But in the midst of all the celebration, I began waking each morning with the feeling, *I'm exhausted already. I'm gonna need a nap today.* That's understandable after a big event like a wedding, a big party, or hosting a conference, but a person should bounce back after a few days of rest. I was not bouncing anywhere. I struggled with fatigue. It's hard to say whether it started as physical exhaustion and became emotional weariness, or the other way around. Doing even simple tasks each day became an emotional drain, and my focus grew shaky.

I started to think, *Why can't I get refreshed? Why can't I get my energy back? This is exhausting, all this inhaling and exhaling. Am I experiencing burnout?*

After I told Holly that I thought I'd hit a physical or an emotional wall, we decided to take some time off. It was a poorly planned and feeble attempt at a sabbatical to regain my strength.

Then a few months later, in March 2014, Holly's dad died. Jim Roberts was a great dad, a successful business executive, and a really good man. He was a dad to me in ways that my own father could not be. He always had a specific word of encouragement for me as I pursued my dreams. Holly and I deeply ached over the loss.

While we were dealing with that grief, a man on our church staff who had worked for us for just a few months informed us he wanted to start his own church. He used the platform we had entrusted him with to rally people to his new church.

Then all of a sudden, Los Angeles became *the* place to plant a church, and a few churches were started within minutes of ours. Los Angeles is a big place with millions of people who need to know Jesus, so we definitely need more churches, but many people left Oasis to try out the new church on the block. We lost about five hundred people in a one-month period. My dream was taking hit after hit.

Soon after that we received a call from our personal bookkeeper who raised questions about some strange spending patterns and withdrawals from our bank account. Over the next week Holly and I discovered that a combination of fraud, computer hacking, and identity theft had wiped thirty-five thousand dollars from our savings. After many phone calls to the Los Angeles Police Department, their Computer Crimes division, and the FBI, we were able to recover some of the money, but most of it was already overseas. Gone.

Exhaustion, death, loss, betrayal, fraud—I needed a break. I felt like a boxer who was backed into a corner of the ring after ten rounds and was taking one hit after another: a punch in the stomach, a blow to the head, a jab to the side, and one more to the jaw. It was time for another vacation.

It's a weird feeling when you take a two-week vacation in the Caribbean and it is so relaxing that you realize if you don't get two or three more weeks, you're just not going to make it. That's when I got the physical exam that led to the cancer diagnosis.

The temptation was strong to feel sorry for myself and to question everything. When we face one crisis after another, not only is it easy to ask ourselves what we did to deserve it all and ask God why we are suffering if we are following His will for our lives, it also becomes difficult to find the energy and focus to continue to pursue our dreams. What do we do when the hits keep coming and the dream starts to fade?

## When Trouble Keeps Coming

I thought fighting cancer would be my biggest battle, but I had no idea what the next few months would hold. I went on a strict regimen including physical and spiritual therapies. Jordan Rubin, author of *The Maker's Diet,* gave me personal guidance and support. I made my own green drinks by blending fresh juices. I took a daily forty-minute, hundred-and-thirty-degree sauna. And I read and prayed daily over a list of scriptures about the healing power of Jesus Christ.

Although much of my prayer, faith, and alternative methods greatly reduced the tumor on my scalp, we decided to do chemo. It shrank the tumor immediately.

One rainy Thursday morning in January 2015, my ears told me what my brain was hesitant to accept. "I see no trace of cancer," the doctor said. "I think we got it all. Hopefully we will just need to check in every few months from here on out."

That was great news to hear!

"I've turned a corner. Finally!" I told several friends. "Now I'm going to start feeling great again."

But just a few days later I experienced intense pain in my legs, I had no energy, and I felt worse than ever. *Why am I not bouncing back?* I wondered.

I saw my doctor, who told me, "You have shingles."

My immediate-comeback plans vanished. Apparently while the chemo worked to make my tumor disappear, it did the same to my immune system. Wiped out! Physically, I was about to have the worst five weeks of my life. I don't want to sound overly dramatic, but I started comparing myself to Job, clearly too far of a reach.

I ended up being out of my normal work schedule for about a year.

"I have a new strategy," I announced to Holly. "I'm going to take a six-month vacation! Twice a year." I tried to keep lighthearted about everything, but the truth wasn't too far from that statement. For most of 2015 I preached only once a month and then spent a couple days in bed recovering. It felt like all these crises weren't just affecting my health and energy; they were affecting my dreams.

I struggled to get my immune system strong again. I tried to regain physical and spiritual strength and stamina. I watched helplessly as the church I loved and had dreamed about lost momentum, even though we continued to reach many people for Jesus.

When I finally returned full time to work in August 2015, I got hit again. This time, in a strange series of transitions, church members and friends who had been part of our church for years chose the moment of my return to move on from Oasis to find another church.

Twenty-five to thirty people, including many leaders, left. Returning to my role as lead pastor and rebuilding the lost momentum in our church got a hundred times harder. Overnight. No one seemed concerned or aware that their immediate and untimely departure multiplied the negative blows to our church and to me as its pastor. In the previous year and a half, our weekend attendance went down from three thousand to two thousand.

I kept feeling as though I'd walked in thirty minutes late to a movie only to wonder, *What's going on here? Did I miss something?* I'd endured a year of grasping for fresh energy and thought I was now going to enter an invigorating season of faith, renewed vision, and trust, that my dream was going to be empowered and strengthened. That was not to be. Not yet.

It was almost impossible not to take some of this trouble as a personal rejection. I felt abandoned by those I had given so much of my heart to. But I knew I couldn't quit my God-dream. I focused on the great people who were still in our church and on our leadership team. So many people were being saved and experiencing dramatic life change because of an encounter with Jesus. I studied Paul's struggles that he wrote about in 2 Corinthians:

> We are pressed on every side by troubles, but we are not crushed. We are perplexed, but not driven to despair. We are hunted down, but never abandoned by God. We get knocked down, but we are not destroyed. Through suffering, our bodies continue to share in the death of Jesus so that the life of Jesus may also be seen in our bodies.
>
> Yes, we live under constant danger of death because we serve Jesus, so that the life of Jesus will be evident in our dying bodies. . . .
>
> But we continue to preach because we have the same kind of faith the psalmist had when he said, "I believed in God, so I spoke." We know that God, who raised the Lord Jesus, will also raise us with Jesus and present us to himself together with you. All of this is for your benefit. And as God's grace reaches more and more people, there will be great thanksgiving, and God will receive more and more glory.
>
> That is why we never give up. Though our bodies are dying, our spirits are being renewed every day. For our present troubles are small and won't last very long. Yet they produce for us a glory that vastly outweighs them and will last forever! So we don't look at the troubles we can see now; rather, we fix our gaze on things that cannot be seen.

For the things we see now will soon be gone, but the things we cannot see will last forever.[2]

"I may not be an actual Christian," I said out loud after reading this Scripture passage. Paul had been beaten multiple times, shipwrecked, imprisoned. He went through all that and yet his faith was strong. I began to declare,

- "I am not crushed. I am not driven to despair."
- "I get knocked down, but I am not destroyed."
- "I believed in God, so I speak."
- "My spirit is being renewed every day. My present troubles are small and won't last."
- "I don't look at the troubles I see; I fix my gaze on things that cannot be seen."

I started to recognize that the crises we face will either bury us and our dreams or carry them to greater heights. As a quote often attributed to C. S. Lewis reminds us, "Hardships often prepare ordinary people for an extraordinary destiny." And author and cancer survivor L. R. Knost puts it this way:

Life is amazing. And then it's awful. And then it's amazing again. And in between the amazing and the awful it's ordinary and mundane and routine. Breathe in the amazing, hold on through the awful, and relax and exhale during the ordinary. That's just living heartbreaking, soul-healing, amazing, awful, ordinary life. And it's breathtakingly beautiful.[3]

## A Faith That Transcends Tragedy

The most powerful lesson I learned during those two years of crisis after crisis was that the faith inside me has to be greater than the circumstances I face.

One of the hardest parts of life is dealing with the tragedies, heartbreaks, and losses we experience. We can become so obsessed and overwhelmed with simply trying to survive that we can easily push our dreams away and stop focusing on them.

> *Often it's in our darkest moments that we begin to develop the ability to succeed over adversity.*

*How do I make it through this day?* I thought many times.

Maybe you've wondered, *How do I get through these times with my faith intact?* If you have thought this, you are normal. Sometimes the only way *out* of the valley is *through* the valley.

I believe, though, that often it's in our darkest moments that we begin to develop the ability to succeed over adversity. Understanding that reality will be more useful than you may want to think about when it comes to unlocking your dreams. I have known men and women who, even though they may have been temporarily broken, found a way to live out of a faith that transcends the crises they faced. They experienced comfort, strength, and peace—a peace that passes all understanding. This happened because they made choices that led them back to a place of strength and hope.

I've met people who have experienced rape or sexual abuse but have found faith deep inside them to overcome. I've talked with people who have been through a financial collapse, lost a job, or failed at their business. I've witnessed families endure a son killed in a tragic event, a baby who died, and a young mother who died and left her children behind. These are devastating experiences. These things often paralyze dreamers so that our hearts go on lockdown.

Something about our faith in Jesus brings hope and courage. We must discover a level of faith that brings a resource to our lives we never imagined was there. What's that level of faith? It's about embracing grace. I've seen it rise up in the middle of the ashes, a certainty that our suffering doesn't escape the eyes of our Creator and Redeemer. He knew we would experience these tragedies when He planted God-dreams within us. He desires for our faith to bring us through those troubles.

In crisis we can discover a key to keeping our dreams unlocked and alive: our faith in His grace. "His grace is more than enough for me," I've heard myself say, paraphrasing 2 Corinthians 12:9. Then I remind myself, *I did not realize until I was in the middle of the fire that God gave me the strength. Heaven's strength overcame my weaknesses, and somehow I know I* will *make it through this.*

David wrote that "the Lord is close to the brokenhearted; he rescues those whose spirits are crushed."[4] We have that same hope and strength to conquer under any circumstances and to turn our pain into purpose.

"I choose to trust God with my dreams in the middle of my pain." The first time I said that, it didn't feel genuine. As I continued to declare my faith in Him, my trust in God grew. My faith got stronger. Jesus came into our world to overcome the darkness, despair, rejection, and loneliness we feel. He experienced the poverty, grief, torture, and imprisonment humanity faces.

Don't give up because of one bad chapter in your life. Keep going. The story does not end here. That knowledge alone can build your faith and keep your dreams alive.

I would often use these scriptures to guide me as I prayed. They helped me keep my hopes higher than my circumstances.

- He personally carried our sins in his body on the cross so that we can be dead to sin and live for what is right. By his wounds you are healed. (1 Peter 2:24, NLT)
- He has delivered us from such a deadly peril, and he will deliver us again. On him we have set our hope that he will continue to deliver us. (2 Corinthian 1:10)

- Let us hold tightly without wavering to the hope we affirm, for God can be trusted to keep his promise. (Hebrews 10:23, NLT)
- The thief comes only to steal and kill and destroy; I have come that they may have life, and have it to the full. (John 10:10)
- A cheerful look brings joy to the heart; good news makes for good health. (Proverbs 15:30, NLT)
- I know the plans I have for you . . . plans for good and not for disaster, to give you a future and a hope. (Jeremiah 29:11, NLT)
- The LORD your God turned the curse into a blessing for you, because the LORD your God loves you. (Deuteronomy 23:5, NKJV)
- Praise the LORD, my soul, and forget not all his benefits . . . who redeems your life from the pit and crowns you with love and compassion, who satisfies your desires with good things so that your youth is renewed like the eagle's. (Psalm 103:2, 4–5)

These scriptures helped me focus on what I really believe. If we don't stick to our values when we're tested, they aren't actually values; they're just hobbies.

> *We will be marked by the past, or we can use it to leave a mark on the future.*

In His death, Jesus suffered in His love, identifying with the abandoned and the forsaken He came to save. We find strength and courage to face even the most brutal of realities because God is still with us. We will be marked by the past, or we can use it to leave a mark on the future.

Pastoring Oasis for more than thirty years, over and over I hear the courageous stories of dreamers who have gone through the darkest times to say later that God was with them. I hear the stories of people who say, "I want to help others who are going through what I've been through." Dreamers want to help others who dream. That's turning pain into purpose—and that's part of every God-dream.

We can try to bury our sorrows in addictions or allow our hearts to be enlarged by the same things that break them. We can allow our wounds to fester and we can become angry, or we can choose to be grateful even when there seems to be little reason for it. We can get smaller or larger in our responses. We can be consumed by pain or become compassionate for others who are facing the same storms. Be bitter or be better. There is a choice to make if you want to keep your dream alive.

The keys that unlock the dream that crisis has put on the shelf are trusting God in the middle of the storms, trusting God after the waters recede, and rediscovering hope that comes from heaven's touch in our circumstances. In the end, the decision to continue obeying God is one of the strongest decisions we can make.

As you pursue your dream, you will inevitably encounter obstacles. You will very likely even face crises that threaten to derail your life, not to mention the dream you are going after. If you get locked in a cycle of feeling sorry for yourself, getting sucked into despair, or letting your doubt overtake your faith and confidence in what God has promised, you won't unlock your dream. If you can take what you experience and allow it to strengthen you and even turn it into a lesson that will help you empower other dreamers, the struggle you endure could turn out to be one of the best things that's happened for your dream.

| | |

**DREAM LOCK:** Going through a crisis can cause you to question your faith and God, allowing your pain to derail you from your God-dreams.

**DREAM KEY:** Move toward God in a crisis instead of drawing away from Him, learn from your circumstances, turn pain into purpose, and develop an ability to conquer under any situation.

**SCRIPTURE KEY:** This I declare about the LORD: he alone is my refuge, my place of safety; he is my God, and I trust him. For he will rescue you from every trap and protect you from deadly disease. He will cover you with his feathers. He will shelter you with his wings. His faithful promises are your armor and protection. . . . If you make the LORD your refuge, if you make the Most High your shelter, no evil will conquer you. (Psalm 91:2–4, 9–10, NLT)

# Betrayal's Burden

> The saddest thing about betrayal is that it never comes from your enemies; it always comes from those you trust.
>
> —UNKNOWN

Looking into the hurting eyes of a person whose spouse has been unfaithful or who has been betrayed by a trusted friend is a difficult thing. I have compassion for the person's pain, and I try to give comfort or hope. When I hear about the pain that disloyalty has caused in someone I know well, the sadness is more personal because I know the devastation of betrayal goes deep.

Few disappointments are more paralyzing than betrayal. In order to completely unlock our dream, it is vital to find a way to *get past what we may never get over.* Getting past the pain with our faith intact is an added struggle on top of the journey itself. We need more than just our faith intact; we need a faith that frees us from the past.

Getting past a hurt is not just forgetting about it. It is about finding enough freedom from that pain to pursue our dreams without the stinging memory of heartbreaks and without the limiting impact of old wounds. It requires a faith that isn't shaken even though life doesn't go smoothly.

Dealing with betrayal is a burden no one signs up for. Yet enduring hurt and loss are common experiences that, if we don't resolve them in a healthy way, can keep us chained to the pain. We can erase someone's betrayal from our minds, but getting the hurt out of our hearts is another story. Sometimes we can resolve the conflict or accept the misunderstanding so we can forgive and move forward. The difference between moving *forward* and moving *on* is massive.

Moving *on* means you've found the energy to keep going, living and surviving. Moving *forward,* however, includes finding healing from the hurts, resolving inner conflicts, and living at a higher level. Many people find a way to keep busy with life—working, building friendships, or even volunteering in the community—but inside they carry a deeply buried wound. It is possible to look at that pain, express it, and find a way to resolve it so that you can move forward. You can live free from unconsciously harboring debilitating bitterness if you will choose between yesterday and tomorrow. Do you want your story to be about the past or about the dream you are pursuing?

Joseph the dreamer sat in a pit wondering about his future. His brothers had betrayed him and taken everything from him. They wanted to kill him, but instead they "compromised" on that idea and came up with plan B, which was to sell him into slavery.[1]

The Bible doesn't tell us how Joseph processed this betrayal. We don't know how he navigated his emotions. We do know he not only survived; he prospered. He learned how to move forward out of betrayal's grasp to a place where his dream could flourish.

Since you are alive and breathing, you too have probably been betrayed. Somebody close to you promised to do one thing, then deceived you by not doing it or even by doing something completely different. The pain of that act can shut down your ability to fully experience your dreams. Learning to move forward out of betrayal is an important key for unlocking your dreams.

## An Experience of Betrayal

Several years ago I hired David* to help us strengthen some weaker areas in our church's structure and to assist me in developing leaders who could take our church into the next level of growth. David was a former lead pastor and had more than twenty-five years of ministry experience. I believed him to be a trustworthy man who would be fully content in the number two position of the church pastoral staff. After interviews, reference checks, prayer, and many conversations, we offered him the position.

He affirmed our belief when he told me, "It's clear to me that God is leading me here. There is nowhere I'd rather be. I'm honored that you would entrust your life work to me. I believe God wants me to finish my ministry years here, serving your vision. It's a dream come true."

David's position carried with it crucial responsibilities. He was the main teacher any time I was absent, oversaw leadership meetings, taught our future leaders in our internship program, and ministered to our staff. We spent many hours and thousands of dollars as we worked through a strategic plan involving him in this key role.

David's arrival seemed like a God thing because after he'd been there a few months, as I was still reeling from the weariness of moving into our new building and feeling exhausted from all the pressures of doing ministry for thirty years, I took an overdue eight-week leave of absence to get refreshed for the next ministry phase. I left the platform and leadership responsibilities to him and others on the leadership team.

When I returned from my break, David informed me, "I believe that God wants me to plant a new church." All the energized feelings from my time of refreshment were sucked out of the room. The sound of it was deafening.

---

* Not his real name.

"You are putting us in a really difficult place," I told him, considering the weight of my words. "I trusted you with my dream, my life's work. I gave you a place in people's hearts."

He was suddenly interested in his shoes.

"David, you said God was leading you here for the next ten or twelve years. Are you saying God changed His mind? Either God was leading you to our church at first and now you have created your own plans for what you want to do, or God was *not* leading you before and *now* you are hearing God clearer. But it can't be both. At least acknowledge that you messed up in representing what God was telling you at some point along this journey."

Insert the sound of crickets chirping here.

"I would never do or say anything to take Oasis's people to my new church. I will do everything I can to make sure they do not follow me," David said, trying to reassure me.

Within two months David was on a mission to start his church, and without regard for his promises, he hired one of our staff members, along with a former and very popular leader from our church. Soon more people followed him away from Oasis.

The next betrayal unfolded. "*God is leading* me to start in a place about twenty minutes' drive from here," he informed me. In LA that is a short drive time.

"What about the ministry agreement you signed when you were hired? It states that if you leave, you will not start or be involved in any church leadership within forty minutes of our church. That was established to protect the church, Oasis, where you are currently serving."

"I don't remember signing that, but I do know that God is leading me to do this," he said.

Clearly, David was going to disregard any agreements so he could have enough people for a solid start. He began a journey of dishonesty and deception that could not have been more destructive.

Friendships were broken, awkward conversations and rumors ran through the church, and many of our leaders suffered great hurts. All the things that I had hoped to avoid by hiring someone *not* driven by ambition came raining down upon me, our church, and my dream.

"I trusted him," I vented to a confidant.

"I know you did," my friend replied.

"I can't believe he did that to me. He stabbed me in the back. Literally."

"Literally?"

"Well, not literally. That would be a felony," I said. "But it feels like it."

That night I talked to a pastor friend. He reassured me and gave me some welcome advice. "We've all been through this before and will probably go through it again. You will be okay. It doesn't feel like it now, but you will."

Later, sitting with my wife and staring at the wall in our darkened living room, I finally conceded, "I don't think I can take this anymore. This is too hard." I even thought, *Maybe I can get my old job back as a software salesperson or that limo driver position . . .*

I had never felt more like quitting my dreams. Every emotional issue that I've ever had, or thought I may have, surged to the surface, racing out of former insecurities like dogs do when you open the back door to let them run. I experienced despair, a little shame, and anger with some confusion, distrust, and depression piled on.

People left Oasis—family after family and friend after friend—over the next few weeks. Friendships broke apart that would never mend. Some people left the church never to return to any church—ever.

Unrelenting questions bombarded my brain. *Is the bleeding ever going to stop? Can I ever trust people again? Could I get Michael Franzese, a former Mafia boss who's now a Christian, to be on our board of directors?*

Conversation after conversation began with, "I really love Oasis and all that the church has done for me. I don't know where my life would be without this ministry"—the ending was always the same—"but I'm leaving the church."

The next few months were about as stress free as walking through a minefield. In spite of the pain, I showed up each Sunday. We prayed and worshiped. We taught God's Word and led people to Jesus. And a miracle happened. People kept coming. I was reminded once again that it is Jesus who builds His church. Through every transition, especially the painful ones, God is faithful to make us stronger than we were before.

> *Love denied blights the soul we owe to God.*
> —William Shakespeare, *Shakespeare in Love*

Mine is a story that could be told a thousand different times by a thousand different leaders and all that would change is a detail or two and the names of the people involved. The previous reliance on God speaking to us in "whispers" seems to be replaced with painful silence. David's betrayal left me pastoring through the pain. If you've been through this kind of betrayal, you are not alone. I've tried to keep a tough skin and a soft heart. It's a difficult balance to maintain. You can't lead well with the opposite—soft skin and a hard heart. Having tough skin, not taking everything so personally, is easier said than done. Many times we find ourselves in survival mode, trying to endure.

Most people have no idea what is going on in your heart and mind, the places where you make your tough decisions, even though those people may speak as if they do.

The ability to keep a soft and compassionate heart is essential. To continue to love what you do and whom you are doing it for can be a challenge, but it's key if your dream is to survive.

## Keep Your Dream Intact

When someone threatens to derail our dreams and when we face heart wounds, we can go on an emotional lockdown. It's difficult enough to protect ourselves and navigate the accusations our own minds throw at us, never mind the accusations other people may throw our way.

In the movie *Shakespeare in Love,* Will says, "Love denied blights the soul we owe to God." We cannot afford to make that mistake. Our task becomes finding wholeness for our souls so our hearts can be fully available to God. There is no new remedy. It's the same old medicine for renewal that has brought breathtaking, life-altering results throughout the ages: forgiveness and refreshment.

It was 4:00 a.m. and I couldn't sleep. My mind kept reviewing the heart-wrenching details of the betrayal. I began to imagine dark wishes on my enemies: a long life of dinner tables with uneven legs, spider bites between their toes, and continual hacked e-mail accounts—weekly.

The longer I lay there, the more my mind blew the incident out of proportion. I had awful thoughts that I don't want to say out loud because they would make my guardian angel drink wine straight out of the bottle. Finally, something in my spirit blew the whistle on me. *This is not helping,* I realized. *I'm poisoning my own spirit now. How can I possibly pursue the dream God has given me by holding on to these bitter feelings?*

I knew what I had to do, and it didn't involve spider bites. I had to forgive. Refocus. Heal. Trust. Refresh. Rinse. And repeat! If you want to keep your dream from becoming derailed, you'll need to do the same.

### Forgive

The first thing I did that helped me move forward was to acknowledge how much the betrayal hurt. I confessed not just to God but to safe people. I met with a counselor and spoke to a friend, talking through the disappointments and the feelings of loss. We prayed together for the healing of my heart.

I had to forgive. Really forgive. Not just say the words but *mean them*. It starts as a decision. The decision doesn't always bring immediate relief. It's the *process* that we commit to. When we forgive, we give up the idea that the past will be different from how it actually was.

I began to forgive David and the others who had followed him. It was a decision of my will at first, but over time it became heartfelt. He left the church he planted after several months to join another church staff, claiming God was leading him again, and I felt the sting of the needless loss of friends I loved. I couldn't control what he had done, but I knew that even though I'd experienced that betrayal, it didn't have to affect my dream.

### Refocus

During that time I learned to find things of value to focus on. People were leaving our church, but others were coming to know Jesus in a real way. Ministry was still happening. God was still moving. My dream was still alive, even if wounded. As long as I focused on those things, I was able to let go of the anger. Sometimes memories are the worst form of torture. I had to refuse to allow them to linger in my mind. If they showed up, I *chose* to replace them with something better. The apostle Paul encouraged us to think about "whatever is true, whatever is noble, whatever is right, whatever is pure, whatever is lovely, whatever is admirable—if anything is excellent or praiseworthy—think about such things. . . . *And the God of peace will be with you.*"[2]

### Heal

Ask God for healing. Recognize that wounds of this kind are beyond our own ability to heal. Not only did I feel my trust violated; I was concerned about the impact David's actions would have on the ministry we were building. I worried that this decision would negatively impact new believers and those who were innocently caught in the middle. His decision to take the opportunity I entrusted him with and parlay it into a chance to influence people was not setting a good example of Christian leadership for them.

I realized it was out of my hands and in God's hands to bring healing to my heart and to the lives of those influenced by David's actions. It was also fully in God's ability to use this circumstance to draw all of us closer to Him and turn it into something good.

### Trust

Ask for the Holy Spirit's help in learning to trust again. We trust some and then trust some more. This is when healing begins to make a deeper impact in our souls. The writer of Hebrews told us to "make every effort to live in peace with everyone" and to "see to it that no one falls short of the grace of God and that no bitter root grows up to cause trouble and defile many."[3] Trust does not come easily after betrayal, and there is no simple formula for being able to trust again. A lot of the work required for regaining trust is the responsibility of the person who damaged the relationship, but we, the injured, have to be open to repairing the trust and restoring the relationship. It is important to understand that not all relationships can be restored and not all people can earn the right to be trusted again. But we cannot make any real progress there without our willingness to trust again, even if it's one "trust step" at a time.

### Refresh

Being refreshed happens with time and effort. Rest and distance from the situation can help us find the space to discover renewed energy and passion for pursuing our God-dream. We decide. We get renewed vision. We practice. We choose. We don't allow betrayals to steal from us. When we intentionally refresh ourselves, we grow stronger.

*Repeat*

We can remove someone from our minds. Getting them out of our hearts is another story. So when the pain returns—and it will—forgive, refocus, heal, trust, and refresh all over again. #RinseAndRepeat. I repeat this cycle until the pain fades.

Remembering who we really are keeps our souls on course. No matter how much our hearts ache, if we keep believing that God put that dream in us for a reason—and that reason hasn't changed—then that conviction and hope will give us the strength to carry on.

You can tell yourself what I told myself:

*I can do this.*

*I will make it through this season.*

*No weapon formed against me will prosper.*

*My God is faithful. He is not finished with me.*

*The best is yet to come.*

## Anger Alone Does Not Remove the Pain

In the movie *Forrest Gump,* Forrest's lifetime love, Jenny, had endured a childhood of sexual and physical abuse at her father's hands. The pain of this abuse led her to make horrible decisions throughout her life, which piled on more hurt and abuse. As Forrest narrates the story in his naive way, they return to the abandoned house where she experienced the abuses. Her rage rises to overflowing, and she begins to cry and throw rocks at the old house.

Forrest explains to the audience, "Sometimes there just aren't enough rocks."

Wounds unhealed carry with them anger, rage, and more heartbreak. We have to deal with this debilitating anger. Expressing anger alone will not make the hurt fade. Being angry feels better for a short time, but then we realize, as Forrest did, *sometimes there just aren't enough rocks.* Healing inner hurts takes time and it takes work. It's the kind of work that dreamers are willing to do because it unlocks our souls.

To use another movie example, *42* showed the life of Jackie Robinson and the painful and unrelenting prejudice he encountered in becoming the first black major league baseball player. In the movie, the Dodgers' general manager, Branch Rickey, was trying to convince Jackie not to fight back when he was insulted. Rickey wanted him to show his "fight" by how he played on the baseball diamond.

> JACKIE ROBINSON: "You want a player who doesn't have the guts to fight back?"
> BRANCH RICKEY: "No. I want a player who's got the guts *not* to fight back."

If we allow our anger to live inside us—because we believe that since we've been hurt, we deserve the right to do so—then not only will we fail to heal; we will crush any chance our dreams have of becoming the full version of what God meant them to be. Don't let anger lock up your dreams.

### Extreme Forgiveness

I have mentioned the importance of forgiving others, but it's important enough that I want you to see the power of forgiveness through the story of Corrie ten Boom.

In May 1940, the German army came though the Netherlands and began to Nazify the Dutch people. Corrie ten Boom and her family refused to give in. They responded by risking their lives to harbor Jews, students, and intellectuals that the Gestapo was hunting. They built a secret room in their home, no larger than a small closet, behind a false wall in Corrie's bedroom, so they could hide Jewish people who were trying to escape. The space could hold six people.

In February 1944, a Dutch informant told the Nazis about the ten Booms' work, and the Nazis arrested the entire ten Boom family and sent them to Scheveningen prison. Two of Corrie's siblings, sister Nollie and brother Willem, were released, along with Corrie's nephew, Peter. But Corrie's father, Casper, died ten days later, and Corrie and her sister Betsie were shipped to Ravensbrück concentration camp in Germany. Betsie died there in December. Corrie was finally released on December 28, 1944, due to a "clerical error."

After the war ended Corrie traveled the world speaking about God's faithfulness. She also wrote about her experiences in the best-selling book *The Hiding Place,* which also became a movie.

I had the opportunity to hear her speak several times. I was always moved by this woman, who was by then in her eighties, and how she talked about her simple but profound faith in God. One story she shared dealt with betrayal and forgiveness.

Three years after she was released, and after the war had ended, Corrie was speaking in Germany. Afterward, a man in a gray overcoat approached her. Immediately she knew who he was. He had been a guard at her concentration camp.

"You mentioned Ravensbrück in your talk," he was saying. "I was a guard there." No, he did not remember me.

"But since that time," he went on, "I have become a Christian. I know that God has forgiven me for the cruel things I did there, but I would like to hear it from your lips as well. Fraulein,"—again the hand came out—"will you forgive me?"[4]

She stood there. After she had given a talk about forgiveness, she now found herself struggling with that very issue. She thought about her sister Betsie who had died in that camp. Even if Corrie forgave him, it wouldn't change that fact—or her grief over it. She wrestled in her mind and spirit about how to respond. She didn't want to forgive him. In her heart she held a coldness toward him. But deep down, she knew she must accept his request and forgive.

> I had to do it—I knew that. The message that God forgives has a prior condition: that we forgive those who have injured us. "If you do not forgive men their trespasses," Jesus says, "neither will your Father in heaven forgive your trespasses." . . .
>
> Forgiveness is not an emotion—I knew that too. Forgiveness is an act of the will, and the will can function regardless of the temperature of the heart. "Jesus, help me!" I prayed silently. "I can lift my hand. I can do that much. You supply the feeling."
>
> And so woodenly, mechanically, I thrust my hand into the one stretched out to me. And as I did, an incredible thing took place. The current started in my shoulder, raced down my arm, sprang into our joined hands. And then this healing warmth seemed to flood my whole being, bring tears to my eyes.
>
> "I forgive you, brother!" I cried. "With all my heart."[5]

Wow.

If Corrie ten Boom could forgive the Nazis for killing her family and imprisoning and degrading her in a concentration camp, then you and I have the capacity to forgive those people who have said hurtful things about us, have failed to keep promises, or even have broken up friendships. One thing I can tell you for sure, the road to dreams fulfilled is traveled by those who have learned to forgive, let go, heal, and move forward.

## The Secret Wounds of Jesus

Jesus was bitterly betrayed. He is our example on how to move forward. A friend of mine talks about "the secret wounds" of Jesus. He refers to the kiss that Judas gave Him in the garden of Gethsemane. Judas was a disciple, one of Jesus's friends. "A crowd approached, led by Judas, one of the twelve disciples. Judas walked over to Jesus to greet him with a kiss. But Jesus said, 'Judas, would you betray the Son of Man with a kiss?'"[6]

This was one big betrayal. Earlier in the Gospels, we learn that Jesus knew this was coming. That's a giant advantage Jesus had over you and me. He knew. I'm usually taken by surprise. As if I've been rear-ended by an eighteen-wheeler truck.

Jesus was betrayed again, this time by another close friend. Peter denied—three times—even knowing Him.

And still He was betrayed again. Earlier that week as Jesus entered Jerusalem, the people had shouted their praise and admiration.

> When he came near the place where the road goes down the Mount
> of Olives, the whole crowd of disciples began joyfully to praise God in
> loud voices for all the miracles they had seen:
>> "Blessed is the king who comes in the name of the Lord!"
>> "Peace in heaven and glory in the highest!"[7]

Less than a week later, as Jesus was subjected to a mock trial, some of these same people stood in the crowd and yelled, "Crucify him! Crucify him!"

We have seen the movies that portray the crucifixion: the beatings, the crown of thorns, the spear in His side, all the suffering He endured leading to His death. I wonder, If we could see the wounds that are not visible to the natural eye, would we see how they too played a big part in His death?

Jesus understands the pain and deep anguish that come from betrayal: "Father, forgive them, for they don't know what they are doing."[8]

We think that the mess that we've endured will somehow keep us from our God-given dreams. But God has a way of turning our mess into our message, our pain into our purpose. Allowing betrayal to put our hearts on lockdown will prevent us from fully reaching our dreams. Letting go, forgiving, refusing to hold on to hurt and bitterness, and moving forward are not things most people can do on their own. It takes trusting God and His promises.

Jesus offers you a better way to live. He doesn't promise that you will never have trouble or pain. He does promise that He will lead you through it. Nothing can stop you if you trust Him.

God has given you a dream. Whatever that dream is, you cannot allow betrayal's burden to make you give in and give up. The consequences are too great. The world needs you to move forward.

|||

**DREAM LOCK:** Unforgiveness poisons your dreams, and bitterness keeps you from having the full dose of joy that you need.

**DREAM KEY:** When you acknowledge hurts and loss and when you open your heart to allow freedom from that pain, you can move past the events to experience healing.

**SCRIPTURE KEY:** Get rid of all bitterness, rage, anger, harsh words, and slander, as well as all types of evil behavior. Instead, be kind to each other, tenderhearted, forgiving one another, just as God through Christ has forgiven you. (Ephesians 4:31–32, NLT)

# I'll Have What They're Having

> One night Joseph had a dream, and when he told his brothers about it, they hated him more than ever.
> —Genesis 37:5, NLT

"This is where Philip is a *genius*," Holly declared to a small gathering of people. "He can think of things to say in awkward moments that make it funny."

I love being called a genius. I've always suspected that I have more going on inside me than others realize. So naturally, I started comparing myself to Albert Einstein, another genius. I thought about all the similarities I have with him. First, there is the forgetfulness thing. Second, I was not a good student in school, just as Einstein wasn't. I once went out to the mailbox to get our mail and forgot that I was wearing my pajama bottoms. (I've heard Einstein did that.) But this is where the similarities stop.

No one else has actually called me that but Holly. Although there was an A-plus student in high school who once said to me, "Way to go, genius!" But I think he was being sarcastic. He said it after he learned that I'd totally forgotten to prepare for our exam.

I also forget that Holly describes a lot of people in creatively dramatic ways. The day she said that one of our staff members was a genius because of the title he suggested for one of our Connect groups, I realized the term *genius* wasn't as special as I'd thought. Apparently some people just throw that genius label around for all to share.

My point is that comparison is a slippery road. It's human nature to compare ourselves with others, but it can lead to a distorted view of reality that can become lethal to dreamers. There is always someone who is smarter, someone who has more resources, someone who has progressed further in their dream, or someone who has more similarities to Einstein than we do. Let's face it, when I compare myself with Albert Einstein, I will always come up short. On the other hand, I am convinced that he would have made a fairly mediocre pastor, and that's a good place to stop my comparison with him.

Observing how others do what they do can be a great source of inspiration. It motivates me to learn from others and to see what they have accomplished. It inspires me to keep pressing on and staying committed to my dreams. I admire other pastors, writers, dads, husbands, and leaders. I've learned so much from what others have told me they've experienced and the wisdom they've gained in their pursuits.

The inspiring practice of observing and learning from another person's success can quickly descend into the uninspiring trap of comparison. The problem is that there is always someone better at what we do. We can't allow comparison to steal the confidence in our own souls. I think everyone's a genius in some area. But if we compare our weaknesses with another person's strengths, we will always lose in the evaluation.

Comparison can be one of the biggest distractions from following the dream God has for you. Mainly because it's the dream God has for *you*. When you start to compare your progress with other people's, you can confuse *your* assignment with the mission *they* are on—and they *aren't* the same. Comparison can lead to the destructive diversions of jealousy, inferiority, or insecurity. Comparisons unchecked lead us to needless and unrealistic feelings of ingratitude, loneliness, and discouragement. All these symptoms are toxic to our dreams.

A girl says to her still-single girlfriend, "I got engaged! Look at my ring! Isn't this exciting?"

"That's so . . . great . . . I could just cry right now," her friend responds, through her forced smile. She isn't really being honest, mainly because her friend's engagement reminds her how she so desperately wishes she had a boyfriend. She wonders if she will ever be engaged. The comparison trap opens wide its jaws as she forgets about the wonderful, supportive relationships she does have.

We compare ourselves with everyone. We compare ourselves with so many ridiculous things and fail to be grateful for what we have. We compare the place we live with others: "Oh, you sold your big house and got a bigger one? That's nice. I'm just trying to cover rent. It's due tomorrow, by the way." We don't stop to be thankful for having a roof over our heads in the first place.

When comparison is nurtured in the vacuum of our lack of confident identity, it produces the offspring of discontent. When we compare ourselves with others in a way that discourages us, it often comes from a lack of accepting who God made us to be. The greatest challenge to being content is discovering who we are and what we are called to do. The second greatest is being happy with what we find.

## Who Am I? And What Is My Focus?

Not long ago I noticed two young guys standing outside the Abercrombie and Fitch store. They were greeting and welcoming people to the store, some sort of hosts or models. They were bare chested and had abs that were *cut*. Two six-packs. No body fat. Anywhere. These twenty-something-year-old guys were clearly establishing the store's version of cool. I resisted the temptation to stand next to them, pull up my shirt, and compare abs. I may be a dad of twenty-year-olds, but I'm no slouch. Okay, they would probably win that comparison showdown. But *just barely*.

The struggle is real.

As we pursue our dreams, we need to continually remind ourselves of two things: who we are and where our focus needs to be. It's embarrassing to admit how much comparisons affect us. I've even allowed those appraisals to give me a false sense of confidence based on other people's failures and struggles, which reveal other issues I need to deal with.

This deceptive practice of comparison can lead to pride, and pride causes us to feel superior to others when we are not even comparing the same dream or mission. The problem with this approach is that, as inflated as we might feel by seeing others fail, we are equally discouraged by other people's successes.

Jesus had something to say about comparisons. In one story about "bags of gold," He offered us clarity about the importance of being content with what we have been given and keeping that the focus of our responsibility.

In the Matthew 25 parable, Jesus told of a man who went on a trip. Before leaving, he gave his servants portions of his wealth to watch over. One servant received five bags of gold. Another servant received two bags. And one more servant received one bag. The man gave to each according to that servant's abilities.

While the man was away, the servant with five bags of gold invested it, and soon he had five more bags. The same happened with the servant given two bags of gold. He invested it and gained two more bags. The servant with the one bag of gold decided instead to bury the money for safekeeping.

When the man returned from his trip, the servants brought back his wealth. The one with now ten bags of gold explained that he had worked hard to grow the money and had doubled his share.

The man was so pleased he told his servant, "Well done, good and faithful servant! You have been faithful with a few things; I will put you in charge of many things."

The same scene played out for the next servant, who had also doubled his bags, from two to four.

Then the man who had received one bag of gold came. "Master," he said, "I knew that you are a hard man, harvesting where you have not sown and gathering where you have not scattered seed. So I was afraid and went out and hid your gold in the ground. See, here is what belongs to you."

His master replied, "You wicked, lazy servant! So you knew that I harvest where I have not sown and gather where I have not scattered seed? Well then, you should have put my money on deposit with the bankers, so that when I returned I would have received it back with interest.

"So take the bag of gold from him and give it to the one who has ten bags. For whoever has will be given more, and they will have an abundance. Whoever does not have, even what they have will be taken from them."

God gives us talents, skills, abilities, and opportunities. He gives us dreams that are specifically designed for us. We are responsible for what He has entrusted to us. To some He gives those five bags (abilities) and to others He gives two or one, and He has His reasons for doing that. We don't need to understand those reasons in order to fully unlock our dreams. We simply need to know that His reasons are good for us; they are perfect for our purpose and destiny. Genuine trust in God should give us the contentment we need in the pursuit of our dreams. As Martin Luther, a powerhouse leader for the Protestant Reformation, said, "Be content with the calling in which God has placed you."[1]

God will give gifts to others and we just don't understand why. We ask,

"Why do they get five bags? I know they have some character issues. I don't treat people the way they do. I would be much more responsible with what they've been given than they will."

The saying "The grass is always greener on the other side of the fence" points out the common dilemma of comparison but neglects to add the supporting truth that the grass is always greener wherever you water it. It involves work to take care of the grass. The same energy we use to look over the fence in wonder and awe and jealousy could be used to work on our own yard.

When we work with someone, are friends with someone, or know someone who is leading in an area in which we dream to be leading one day, our confidence can be tested. To stand self-assuredly in someone else's shadow requires that we don't allow ourselves to doubt our own capacity while also being free to celebrate someone else's successes. But that requires that we know who we are and have faith in the gifts and dreams God has entrusted specifically to us.

> *Knowing who **you** are is a powerful key to keeping your dream alive. Knowing who you are **not** is equally important.*

The apostle Paul reminds us that "we do not dare to classify or compare ourselves with some who commend themselves. When they measure themselves by themselves and compare themselves with themselves, they are not wise."[2]

Wanting what someone else has indicates ingratitude for what God has given you. It is the same as telling God He doesn't know what is best for you and that He messed up when He gave you your dream.

Peter had the same challenge. After Jesus had been resurrected, He was with His disciples in Galilee and He told Peter what He wanted him to do. Peter was willing, but he was concerned about how that compared to the mission of John, another disciple. Jesus told Peter not to worry about what John was doing. Peter needed just to do what Jesus had asked *him* to do. Jesus said, "If I want him to remain alive until I return, what is that to you? As for you, follow me."[3]

Comparisons will never unlock our dreams to their full potential. Stand strong in the knowledge of who you are and what you've been called to do.

Knowing who *you* are is a powerful key to keeping your dream alive. Knowing who you are *not* is equally important. The clearer we get about who we are, the stronger we are.

When I say we need to know who we are, I'm talking about knowing your strengths, weaknesses, and abilities, knowing what you love to do and what you are good at. It's good to know your weaknesses and accept them, but don't let them limit you. It's important that we don't define ourselves by our—or by other people's—successes or our failures. It's about knowing your value as a person, whether you accomplish all your goals or not. When you know who you are and you also know who you are not, then if you can embrace both, fulfilling contentment will be your reward. Remember, you are defined by what God says about you.

## Breaking Free from the Comparison Con

We all want to matter, and we all want to feel important to people around us. It is a big part of what drives us to our dream. We are searching for significance and want to leave a meaningful mark on the world. But as we've discussed, comparison is a killer of those honorable ambitions and can become a debilitating dream lock.

Here are three keys to help unlock the dreams that have fallen into the comparison trap.

### Key 1: Find Contentment

Contentment means we are completely satisfied with where we are right now and with where we are going. Discontentment leads to wanting what someone else has, and that will be a setback in unlocking our dreams. The practice of comparison weakens our sense of contentment, whereas we discover contentment of the soul through our faith in God. "The LORD is my shepherd, I lack nothing"[4] is God speaking about a secret path to freedom: freedom from wanting more than is good for us; freedom to enjoy and appreciate what we have, where we are, and who and whose we are; and freedom to genuinely wish blessing on everyone we meet.

As Benjamin Franklin once stated, "Content makes poor men rich; discontent makes rich men poor." And the Greek philosopher Epicurus said, "Do not spoil what you have by desiring what you have not; remember that what you now have was once among the things you only hoped for."

It can be challenging to trust that God knows what He is doing when we see others succeeding, even though they don't seem to deserve it or work as hard for it as we do. When we can trust that God made us just the way we are for a very important reason, then we can find our satisfaction in pleasing God and fulfilling the purpose He gave us.

So much of what Jesus taught pointed us toward a level of contentment that is in contrast to our typical pursuit of the *stuff* this world offers. He taught us to find contentment through our faith. Jesus said we can live in unbroken peace and restfulness of soul. If we are not satisfied with what God has given us now, we wouldn't be satisfied if He gave us everything we thought we should have. As the great preacher Charles Spurgeon said, "If you are not content with what you have, you would not be satisfied if it were doubled."

### Key 2: Trust That God Is Guiding You on Your Journey

We don't have the privilege of knowing exactly how we fit into the greater plans God has. Sometimes we get a glimpse of the role we will play, but more often we only know what we are designed to do and don't see the life-changing ripple effect that happens when we step into our purpose.

I mentioned earlier that I once thought I would be a worship leader and that I didn't end up pursuing that. I could have wasted a lot of time pushing toward that dream, insisting it was what I was supposed to do in spite of disappointments and challenges that clearly were telling me I wasn't on the right path. I could have looked at other worship leaders and musicians who were touring and having a big impact for the church, then felt frustrated because I wasn't seeing the same kind of success. That would have kept me from fully stepping into the future God had planned for me.

Comparison will cause you to question whether you are equipped to pursue your God-dream and to stop trusting Him and His love for you. Remember God is not going to set you up for failure by putting you on a path you aren't supposed to follow.

### Key 3: Stay Focused on the Path in Front of You

When our focus is honoring God and the dream He has given us, the comparison struggle comes to an end. Your dream is uniquely tailored for the gifts and talents you have, and it is not something anyone else can fulfill. It is customized just for you and for what God wants you to accomplish.

Our focus needs to be on pursuing the dreams God has for us, not desiring someone else's dreams or opportunities. Our priority must be to seek God's will every step of the way toward *our* dreams. We cannot stay focused on what God desires for us when we are constantly looking over at someone else. When we are so concerned with what someone else has, we lose sight of what we have.

Trusting God and staying focused on what we have been given and gifted with are keys to stopping the distracting temptation of comparison. God gives everyone a dream that is unique to each person. Don't let the comparison trap hold your dreams hostage any longer.

|||

**DREAM LOCK:** Comparison leads either to envy or jealousy; both will put the brakes on your pursuit of the dream and lock you up when you were made to thrive.

**DREAM KEY:** Accept that the God-dream is unique to you as an individual and incomparable to others' dreams.

**SCRIPTURE KEY:** Am I now trying to win the approval of human beings, or of God? Or am I trying to please people? If I were still trying to please people, I would not be a servant of Christ. (Galatians 1:10)

# The Generosity Factor

The world of the generous gets larger and larger; the world of the stingy gets smaller and smaller.
—KING SOLOMON, PROVERBS 11:24, MSG

One important key to unlocking our dreams, which surprises so many dream-chasers, is the quality of generosity. Many people think achieving our dreams means taking, reaching, and striving, and we fail to realize that to fully reach our dreams we will have to increase our capacity to give. It's not just the act of giving that I'm talking about; it's giving generously. I don't mean the simple act of handing a homeless person some loose change or giving to a charity during the holidays. The higher level of giving is generosity— the kind of giving that comes only through a genuine change of heart. It is a transformation of how we approach life. True generosity has to come from a different place than a desire to give what is expected, to appease some social pressure, or just to get a tax write-off. It is about more than money. It has to become a way of life. It means that we give willingly and joyfully, that we give more than is normal.

It seems like we all start from a place where we are worried that if we give what we have to others, we will have less. I'm letting you in on an extraordinary secret. There's more than enough for you. There is more than enough love, there is more than enough time, and there are more than enough resources to reach your dreams. There is more than enough for all of us.

Jesus told us to "give, and it will be given to you."[1] We can trust that God is going to provide everything we need to ensure that we reach our dreams. We can relax our grip on all that we thought would be key to unlocking those dreams. When we really believe this, it's so much easier to be a giver.

Think about the most generous person you've ever known. What impact has that person had on your life? What is a generous act that someone has shown toward you? Was it expressed through that person's kindness, patience, or emotional support? Have you been forgiven for a wrong you committed or an important event that you forgot? Have you received a gift from someone that was larger than you expected? How did this generosity affect you? All these happened because of someone's generosity toward you.

When I was a youth minister, there was a girl in the youth group whose parents owned a computer-software company. They were very supportive of our work with the teenagers. Because we were part of a smaller church with a limited budget, we didn't always have the funds to do all that we wanted to do for the kids. This couple understood that, and so they were generous in their support: they helped us pay for food at youth events and for kids who could not afford to go to camp. They gave of their time and volunteered in many other ways because they wanted those kids to have opportunities to discover a faith in Jesus.

When we started Oasis Church and at times struggled financially, more than once this couple gave funds to help cover the budget. Without their generosity, Oasis would not have the worldwide impact we do today.

Generosity supports and fuels the dreams of others and helps them realize potential they might not be able to access without this kind of encouragement. The generosity we extend to others also plays a role in how we achieve our own dreams, because it sets us up to experience the biblical principle that what we need in life comes to us when we are willing to give to others. God can provide a hundred times more than we have ever given. When we give to others, we plant a seed that will bring a harvest back into our lives, helping us move closer to our own dreams.

## Where Generosity Starts

While this may seem obvious to you, it is a surprise to many people when they realize that God is generous. I didn't think God was generous when I was a young man. Somehow, while growing up, I got the idea that if I begged God for help and if I was good enough, He might show me a little mercy. A lot of people have this belief about God. But God is amazingly generous. He made the first move of generosity toward us.

And the second move and the third.

He was the first and is the most generous Giver of all. He's given us His generous love, generous acceptance and forgiveness, and the generous future that we call the God-dream. Every moment we are alive is a gift from our generous Creator.

He went above and beyond anything we could have imagined: "God so loved the world that *he gave* his one and only Son, that whoever believes in him shall not perish but have eternal life."[2]

God loved people so much that *He gave.* He gave His best. He gave His Son for you and for me. This act of generosity began in His heart first. He loved so He gave.

Once I began to see God's generosity portrayed throughout Scripture, I saw it everywhere:

> When the kindness and love of God our Savior appeared, he saved us, not because of righteous things we had done, but because of his mercy. He saved us through the washing of rebirth and renewal by the Holy Spirit, whom he poured out on us *generously* through Jesus Christ our Savior.[3]

> If any of you lacks wisdom, you should ask God, who gives *generously* to all without finding fault, and it will be given to you.[4]

Jesus pointed out an example of generosity that accentuated the importance of this quality for us. The situation also reveals the heart behind this kind of liberality. He was so taken by it that He said wherever the gospel would be preached, this story would be told.

> *We can give without loving, but we cannot love without giving.*

Jesus was in the home of some friends when a woman came in and poured a very expensive perfume over His head. Jesus's friends and disciples immediately criticized this generosity and declared it wasteful. But Jesus saw it a different way.

> Why criticize this woman for doing such a good thing to me? You will
> always have the poor among you, but you will not always have me.
> She has poured this perfume on me to prepare my body for burial. I
> tell you the truth, wherever the Good News is preached throughout
> the world, this woman's deed will be remembered and discussed.[5]

Her generosity was significant because of the value of her gift: it was a great *sacrifice* and it revealed the depth of her gratitude. Jesus pointed out that this kind of generous gratitude and worship was to be forever connected to His followers.

It's clear that generosity is an irreplaceable quality of spirituality. Inside the soul of every person is a desire that God gave us to live the generous life. Generosity is essential to following Jesus. What Jesus expects us to do in life cannot be done without a generous attitude. Generosity is required to trust God at the depth that produces a life of sacrifice, serving others and even forgiving in the same way we are forgiven. We can give without loving, but we cannot love without giving.

We are most like God when we are generous. Jesus once told His disciples, "By this everyone will know that you are my disciples, if you love one another."[6]

It's important that we love the poor and care for the homeless, but Jesus did not say "they will know we are His disciples" because we feed the poor. It's sometimes easier for us to love strangers than it is to love the people we know because we know their faults and their issues. If people have to deserve what we give, it's not really generosity. We need to show this generous love and grace to people despite their issues. We can only develop a generous life when we understand where giving begins, and that it is with love. This empowers us toward greater heights of generosity.

## How Generosity Changes Us

Generosity continues to transform us in every way. It changes our souls, it changes our views, and it even has an impact on us physically. You might be thinking, *Okay, I get the mental and emotional part, but how does generosity impact me physically?* A hormone called oxytocin, which is also known as the "love hormone" or the "hug hormone," affects our behavior. Research reveals that when we give, we get a shot of oxytocin. Even people who witness someone else's giving can get a boost of oxytocin.

An interesting side effect of oxytocin is that it suppresses the stress hormone cortisol. When we are stressed, we are less generous. When we are stressed, we are less likely to have the feeling of bonding with others. But the more we give, the more oxytocin is produced and the less stress we feel. Science shows that people who are impacted by oxytocin and generosity are more creative, better at problem solving, and have higher degrees of empathy.[7] Can you imagine how much more successful you'd be at pursuing your dreams if your creativity and problem solving were at their peak? Being tuned in to the needs of others and helping them is part of fulfilling our God-dream.

Our souls become more generous when we practice it and when we are intentional in our generosity. Paul tells us,

> Remember this: Whoever sows sparingly will also reap sparingly, and whoever sows generously will also reap generously. Each of you should give what you have decided in your heart to give, not reluctantly or under compulsion, for God loves a cheerful giver. And God is able to bless you abundantly, so that in all things at all times, having all that you need, you will abound in every good work.[8]

It's important that we give because we have decided in our hearts to give. This kind of generosity does not occur because we are under pressure to give. God loves a cheerful giver because people who are happy to give have allowed the Holy Spirit into their souls and allowed Him to transform their hearts so that they express joyful generosity.

## What Generosity Costs Us

Generosity has not come easily to me. I've had to practice giving. I've learned that sometimes we will be called on to make choices and sacrifices, to go places we aren't comfortable going, and to stretch beyond our perceived limitations so we can fulfill what God has asked us to do. In developing generosity in my life, I've learned some lessons about what it means to be authentically generous.

### Lesson 1: Generosity Requires the Willingness to Sacrifice

Everything we have belongs to God. Everything we are is because He has been generous to us. When we live out of those realities, it's easier to keep our hands and hearts open to others with our time, abilities, and resources.

> *I'm convinced that if God knows He can get resources through us to others, He will get more resources to us.*

Remember that God has entrusted us with managing these gifts for Him, that it is a temporary arrangement, and that He has greater plans than we can imagine. He wants us to be available to His guidance and to know we can be trusted to follow through, even if it means diverting resources that He has given us to help someone else. I'm convinced that if God knows He can get resources *through* us to others, He will get more resources *to* us.

### Lesson 2: Generosity Often Creates a Difficult Choice

When we are willing to share what we have, we experience tension between our self-interests and the interests of others. That can present us with a tough decision: *Should I keep this thing or give it to that person?* This is a wonderfully annoying pressure between *I want this for me* and *They need it more.* This tension lets us know that we're considering giving up something that has value. This is another level of sacrifice we are sometimes asked to make in becoming more generous. If it were always easy to give, it would not take faith to be generous. The things that come to us easily don't have the same life-changing impact, and they definitely don't reveal God's provision.

*Lesson 3: Generosity Is Not About Serving Our Own Interests*

While there's nothing wrong with doing something for others knowing that it will increase our lives in return, be careful not to give simply to get something out of it. When we have that attitude, we aren't really giving generously. But when we give to people who don't have something to offer us or when what we give can't possibly be reciprocated, we receive a whole other level of reward: we've pleased God and we've potentially helped them unlock their dreams by giving them a leg up and out of their current situation.

*Lesson 4: One Person's Generosity Inspires Others to Be Generous*

Generous people inspire us. We want to be more like them, so we follow their model and practice generosity. Obviously, as lesson 3 points out, we don't give for the sole purpose of receiving a reward or for having others see us and congratulate us on how generous we are. Jesus taught that it is good to give gifts privately.[9] He also encouraged us to let our giving be an inspiration to others.

One day while He was teaching in the temple, Jesus highlighted the generosity of a very poor woman who gave two small coins as her offering. He compared her gift to the rich people's giving. Her giving was greater or more generous because it cost her more; it was "all she had."[10] We are cautioned not to let our giving become a contest for who can out-give whom, but when we are personally exposed to genuine generosity, we are inspired to a new standard for our own generosity.

*Lesson 5: Generosity Is Powerful Even If the Receiver Is Ungrateful*

There have been times when I've been generous and the one who benefited from it was anything but grateful. Being generous with someone who is not generous with me at a later time is surprising. It can make me wonder if my generosity was worth it. *Why be generous if that person is going to be ungrateful? No good deed goes unpunished,* I might think.

The act of generosity is for our benefit more than for others because God always has a reason to inspire our liberality. We can begin to feel entitled and expect something in return. We are reminded in these situations that generosity is not supposed to be done with expectations for how it will benefit us. God may want us to release something we are holding on to that is keeping us from moving toward our own dreams. King Solomon told us, "The generous will prosper; those who refresh others will themselves be refreshed."[11]

### Lesson 6: We Can Practice Generosity In Our Current Circumstances

We don't get a pass on being generous until we pass some benchmark, acquire a certain amount in savings, or after we get that raise. You may think, *I can't afford to be generous right now.* The truth is, you can't afford not to.

By opening your heart to help meet another's needs, you create the environment where your own needs can be met. Holding back could reveal a lack of trust in God to make up the difference when you give to help others.

### Lesson 7: Generosity Leaves a Legacy

If we focus only on our own lives and our own dreams, we will be limited in our understanding of the potential God has in store for us. Understanding generosity requires seeing beyond just what we need. God has put in you and me the desire to be generous. It's part of God's assignment to us, and if we don't choose generosity, we risk missing out on all that God wants to do in us and through us.

Part of our desire to pursue our dreams is that we want to make a real and lasting difference in the world. Generosity plays a major role in that desire for significance. We may never know what kind of impact we have on others through our generosity, but those gifts will not go unnoticed by God. He will use them far beyond what we could ever hope or imagine . . . or even dream.[12]

In the early 1970s, a young girl named Dorika lived in Kisii, a remote area of Kenya. She had the daily task of walking for miles to find water for her family and bring it back to her home. Dorika went to a local school where, instead of learning, she spent the majority of her time getting water from the river and helping to do chores for teachers. She dreamed of one day going to a real school and learning English and math.

One day something amazing took place. Someone she did not know sponsored her to attend a boarding school in Nairobi, Kenya's capital city, nearly two hundred miles away. This person was looking for a way to give generous support to someone who needed it. Dorika started classes but immediately fell behind in her schoolwork because she didn't speak English, nor had she ever actually experienced learning before. She realized she was going to have to work hard. She began to study harder at her schoolwork than any other student, and by the end of her time there, she graduated first in her class and was able to attend one of the country's top girls' high schools.

Once again someone saw the quality of Dorika's schoolwork and wanted to help her. As the top student in her secondary school's graduating class, she was recognized for the effort she put into her work, so the benefactor decided to extend a random act of generosity and sponsor her to get a first-class college education in the United Kingdom.

This girl who was used to walking miles to find water was now going to the top school in Great Britain. Again she graduated at the head of her class. Yet again, she was sponsored with the opportunity to continue her first-class education, this time at Harvard University. Dorika could not even afford the application fee or the cost of living at school without the generosity of others, but because of it, she received the opportunity of a lifetime.

Before graduating with her MBA from Harvard Business School, she met her husband, Justin. After they were married they moved to Los Angeles, where she became a successful businesswoman. They also began attending Oasis Church. During their time at our church, they met a thirteen-year-old boy who had a drive for business and entrepreneurship. His instincts were compelling and his enthusiasm caught their attention. Dorika's husband, Justin, wanted to mentor this young boy—my son, Jordan.

That thirteen-year-old boy had no idea that eight years later he would lead a charity organization, Generosity.org, and have the opportunity to build a fresh-water well in Kisii, the same village where Dorika grew up.

When we are generous, God uses our gifts to unlock dreams for other people. And those other people then respond by being generous to more people whose dreams get unlocked, and the cycle of generosity continues.

Think about your own dreams. As you pursue them, who has been generous to you in a way that has empowered you to push through? Imagine how many dreams you can unlock—your own and others'—just by opening your heart to becoming a person of generosity.

## Are We Owners or Managers?

There's a story of a man I'll call James, who was in an airport waiting for his plane to depart. He decided to get a coffee and a small bag of doughnuts before his flight. With his coffee and doughnut bag in hand, he returned to the crowded boarding area and sat next to another man who was also waiting for his flight.

James put down his bag, took off his coat, sat, and reached into his bag of doughnuts. He pulled one out and took a bite. To James's surprise the man next to him reached over, took the bag of doughnuts, and took one out also. He ate it and smiled at James.

James couldn't believe this man had just taken one of his doughnuts!

*What's the world coming to?* he thought. He wondered if the man was not right mentally, so he decided against saying anything for fear that the man might go off on him. Instead he kept quiet, but he did give the man a look. You know "the look." When someone behind you is making noise in a theater or in church, and you turn your head slightly to the side and look at the person to communicate your displeasure.

James picked up his bag of doughnuts, grabbed another, and brought the bag a little closer to himself.

Again the man reached over, helped himself to another doughnut, took a bite, and smiled at James.

*I can't believe it! He's done it* twice!

Finally, boarding began and the man got up to leave.

*Hope you enjoyed my doughnuts, you doughnut thief,* James thought.

The man hung his coat over his arm, picked up the bag, reached in, and grabbed the last doughnut. He broke it in half, put one half into his mouth, and returned the other half to the bag, scooting it back over close to James. Then he smiled again and walked away.

*The nerve! This guy is crazy! I'm not touching that doughnut. He probably has some infectious disease.* James crumbled the bag and tossed it into a nearby trash can.

A minute or two later James's boarding section was called, so he stood, grabbed his coat, and reached down to pick up his carrying case. There sitting on top of his case was *his* bag of doughnuts!

James was complaining that the other man was stealing *his* doughnuts when the other man was actually sharing his own with James.[13]

We spend so much time worrying about our own resources, but God owns them all. The "doughnuts" we think we are giving up are actually His. To unlock our dreams, we must be willing to give of ourselves and our assets. When we give freely, we're just giving what God gave us first. He won't cause our dreams to fade away or to be lost.

If we hold back from giving, we will never know the reward that comes from helping someone else and the blessing that happens when we honor God's leading. The fear of not having enough is a major obstacle to living generously and being able to do what God leads you to do. When you can trust that God has you covered and is not going to lead you into something that is harmful for you or your dreams, you will be freer to give generously.

Let your generosity break out so you can open the doors to your dreams and help others open theirs as well.

|||

**DREAM LOCK:** The fear of not having enough can keep you from opening your life to the possibilities that can only be discovered through generosity.

**DREAM KEY:** Look for opportunities to be generous with your time, your talents, and your attention, and for ways to support someone or some cause through financial contributions.

**SCRIPTURE KEY:** Since you excel in everything—in faith, in speech, in knowledge, in complete earnestness and in the love we have kindled in you— see that you also excel in this grace of giving. (2 Corinthians 8:7)

# Being a Dream-Maker

What counts in life is not the mere fact that we have lived. It is what difference we have made to the lives of others that will determine the significance of the life we lead.

— NELSON MANDELA

One of the most famous racehorses in American history was Seabiscuit. His racing career was during the years surrounding the Great Depression. In 1938, Seabiscuit was Horse of the Year. He won eleven of his fifteen races and was the year's leading money winner in the United States. This meant Seabiscuit was worth hundreds of thousands of dollars to his owners.

An intriguing thing about Seabiscuit is that for the first part of his racing career, he was a below-average horse, losing race after race. It appeared to most people in that sport that he was not worth the initial investment. First, he was a small horse, which is not good in the racing world. He had an unimpressive start to his racing career, failing to win his first eighteen races, usually finishing back in the field. His owner, unhappy with his ability, did not spend much time on him and moved his attention to other horses. Seabiscuit just did not live up to his racing potential.

In that sport, there is a race called a claiming race, in which the horses are all for sale before the competition. It is usually a lower-level race, and a buyer can get a horse for a low price. Seabiscuit raced in three claiming races in which he could've been purchased for $2,500, but no buyers were interested. Eventually the owner did manage to sell him so he could buy better horses.

It was a shock to many experts, then, when Seabiscuit *suddenly* became a champion. He was so popular among the people that he became a symbol of hope to many Americans during the Great Depression. For one race at Santa Anita Park, seventy-eight thousand people attended while millions listened on the radio. I guess a lot of people identified with the feeling of an unimpressive showing in life.[1]

This story definitely resonated with me on many levels. The owner and the trainer dreamed about having the greatest horse in the world and winning the big races. Even when everyone doubted that was possible, they banked their hopes on a horse with a very rough start to his racing career. I had a rough start in my life, long on dreams but short on talent. Have you ever felt like that? Have you ever been overlooked by others who did not see your potential? Have you been counted out by those who didn't think you looked or acted the part?

What was behind the complete change in Seabiscuit? A horse trainer who had a unique and unorthodox training style and who nurtured inside Seabiscuit a fire to win. He saw something special in this horse. He kept working with him until he tapped into the hidden potential and unlocked the greatness in him. Without his investment in this horse, we would not be talking about Seabiscuit today.

This story is a reminder that there is something great inside all of us. God created us with a specific purpose to fulfill, and He built us with the ability to do just that. While the God-dream we have is far greater than what Seabiscuit was created to do, he stands as an example of what happens when someone takes the time to look beyond the surface and invest in our potential.

Some people live their entire lives without ever unlocking that great ability God has put inside them. Some start out with a God-given dream and the passion to see that dream fulfilled; it burns in their hearts. But the longer it takes for the dream to come to pass, the less their hearts burn for it and the less they search for it.

We were born to be remarkable, but remarkable does not mean we are better or more successful than everyone else. We don't have to win an Oscar or Businessperson of the Year, sell the most products, or have the largest ministry. Remarkable is defined by what we do, whom we touch, and how we impact their lives. And remarkable can identify any level of dream. Some people think, *I don't want just to raise a family; I want to do something remarkable.* But raising a great family *is* a remarkable dream to attain.

When we talk about reaching our dreams, we tread on sacred territory. Our dreams are so close to our hearts and so important to God. But dreams were never meant to be pursued alone. God so desires for us to reach our dreams that He makes it necessary for us to need others—and for others to need us. In essence, we aren't just dream-pursuers; we're dream-makers.

> *When we help others reach their dreams,*
> *we are forever changed.*

Every person who has ever encouraged me, every song that has inspired me, and every sermon that has put courage in my soul were all dream-makers!

As we attempt to unlock our dreams, we realize that there is one important aspect that, if overlooked, undoes all the rest of the work we've accomplished: the effort we put into helping others reach their dreams. Living generously, as we discussed in the last chapter, is certainly part of that. Another part is embracing and cheering others on. Believing in them, praying for them, and offering them hope. God has a way of taking those offerings and turning them into rewards: they change us into the kind of people who can reach *our* own dreams.

In the movie *The Blind Side,* based on a true story, Leigh Anne Tuohy and her family invested in helping a disadvantaged young boy, Michael Oher, and brought him into their family. Their efforts not only helped him meet his needs, but they prepared him for the future. He was able to go to college and then on to play in the NFL. During one time when they were helping Mike overcome bad grades and a lack of direction, one of Leigh Anne's friends said to her, "You're changing that boy's life." Leigh Anne responded, "No. He's changing mine." That's what happens when we help others reach their dreams: *we* are forever changed.

## The Face of Hope

Twenty-three thousand people every week. That's how many people died of AIDS in 2009, every week of every month.[2]

When I learned those numbers, I felt I had awakened to something going on right around me that I had somehow been blind to! And I couldn't shake the images. Although I was aware of AIDS and the epidemic, somehow the worldwide problems were in other places—and for other people to deal with. I knew that an estimated fifty million children in Africa were orphaned as a result of HIV/AIDS, war, poverty, and disease. So many people had died of AIDS and civil wars that millions of orphans were living in vulnerable circumstances. But that was on the other side of the world.

Instead of thinking, *The problem is too big; I can't do anything about it,* I started to think, *This problem is huge; I've got to do something to help some of those whom this crisis impacts. We can't ignore it.*

This was also around the time when I met Gary and Marilyn Skinner, founders of Watoto Church and Watoto Child Care Ministries in Kampala, Uganda. Uganda was the youngest nation in the world at the time, with 50 percent of its population at fifteen years of age and younger.

Watoto has a children's choir that travels the world as ambassadors of Uganda to raise awareness about the plight of the orphaned and vulnerable children of Africa. They share Watoto's vision and mission through their stories, music, and dance. They sing of their life-changing experiences through Watoto Church and their faith in Jesus.

Each of the children in the choir has suffered the loss of both parents, either through war or disease. Their experience in the choir gives the children exposure to other cultures, broadening their worldview. It also gives them confidence and boldness and helps them rise out of their own sadness and despair.

They live in Watoto's villages. These villages are not what you might think when you hear the word *village*. Many African villages are made up of small huts, flimsy structures with partially effective roofs and trash scattered all around. The villages that Watoto has provided are comprised of homes built with brick and surrounded by a yard with grass that is well maintained and free of litter.[3]

The night I heard them sing, I expected to hear a children's choir and spend a nice little evening enjoying their presentation. But it was so much more than that. Joy and hope came through their voices. That performance changed me. The crisis that I had only read about now had faces connected to it. I said hello to a couple of them after the performance. They hugged me with innocence, and their personal touch went beyond the physical. I knew I would be involved in being part of their dreams.

A year later I had the opportunity to go to Watoto with Holly and our daughter, Paris. We visited their babies' home, originally called the Bulrushes, named after the place the baby Moses was found.[4] Moses had been abandoned but not forsaken; he still had a significant destiny. The Skinners believe that these babies will be Uganda's next generation of great leaders, and they are there to help care for them and train them to make that country great. Their dream is to offer opportunities for these children to grow up and realize *their* God-dreams.

On our first visit to the home, we saw about forty babies, from newborns to eighteen-month-olds. They were adorable, and they loved to be held. One baby stood out to me. She was thin, wore a lifeless expression, and held a distant look in her eyes.

The director told me, "We were called out to a community to pick up an abandoned baby. When we arrived they told us that this other little baby was going to be sacrificed to a local witch doctor and asked if we could take her too, so we brought her to our home." She had only been at the home for a couple of weeks. I asked what her name was, and they said Hope.

For the next several months, I told the story of this little girl and her experience to anyone who would listen. This little girl had the name that sounded like the opposite of her circumstances. A tiny defenseless child who had survived a hopeless situation and whose name was Hope.

When I think about giving hope to others, I think of her little face, the future she can now have, and the dreams she can pursue because someone said yes to giving her that opportunity. Someone became a dream-maker in her life.

When she was moved into one of their children's villages where she could attend school, I became her monthly sponsor. I have visited her five or six times. I've watched her grow and have seen her become a beautiful young lady.

When we help others reach their dreams, it changes our quality of life. But first we must love others. Love causes us to embrace those who are different from us; love demands that we lift those who are pushed down. In the process we become dreamers of what is possible in our own lives. In pursuing my dreams I've figured out that I have to expand my circle of acceptance.

This kind of love is expressed on a larger scale than the love that is directed solely at individuals. It is directed at people who have been marginalized, alienated, or just left out. The process of recognizing our own tendency to dismiss certain groups of humanity changes our hearts. We have to leave our narrowness behind so our capacity can be enlarged. When I expand the type of person I'm willing to love, I include more individuals I can embrace when they come across my path.

For several years, Holly and I have produced a creative and inspirational national women's conference. Originally called GodChicks but now named She Rises, this event has focused on inspiring women around the world, releasing dreams in them by conveying that they are valued and loved. Holly is gifted at proclaiming this message and inspiring women to live with the value that God has put inside them. We hear story after story from women whose lives have been transformed by the message of honor that declares, *You are a loved-beyond-measure daughter of the King.* It's amazing to see what happens when women are in an environment in which they are honored and empowered.

I've been surprised by how many amazing women have gifts that are locked away because of heart wounds and limits that have been imposed on them. But when they are empowered, they unlock their dreams and renew their vision. Part of the journey is to resolve any resentment they feel toward others, including men, because of the injustices and abuse they may have experienced. All people need to be loved. We need to honor others in order for our own dreams to flourish.

Dreams are magnetic and powerful. I didn't discover my life's meaning by looking within myself. I've discovered more about who I am when I've looked around me and tried to help others. That's when I recognize more clearly what my dreams are about.

## Dream-Makers Mentor

In 2012 I received a phone call that I never expected. Sherri Shepherd, one of the cohosts at that time on the TV show *The View,* had been an active member of Oasis Church for several years before she moved to New York. One of the show's producers was on the phone.

She asked if Holly and I would be willing to come on the show as Sherri's guests. January was National Mentoring Month, and they were going to do an episode that focused on mentors. Each host—Whoopi Goldberg, Elisabeth Hasselbeck, Joy Behar, and Sherri—would invite a mentor who had touched her life. Sherri had chosen us.

It was such a strange feeling to be on the show. I knew of all the famous people they'd interviewed, and I kept wondering, *How did we end up in this situation?*

"When I walked into Oasis Church," Sherri told everyone on the show, "I saw this shy, white pastor and his bubbly wife. Pastor Philip may have spoken softly, but his words were powerful. Holly inspired me as a woman, taught me about my value as a woman, and helped me take responsibility for my life. She told me, 'You don't have to be a missionary to make a difference. You just have to touch the lives of people around you.'

"My life changed when I first walked into Oasis. There was a lot of craziness going on in my life. You showed me that faith, hope, and friendship could help you overcome whatever life throws at you. You were nonjudgmental and had a spirit of joy that was contagious. Can you believe my pastors are white?" Everyone laughed. "Why did you invest in me and my life?"

When we first met Sherri, she had lost her faith, she had lost her mom, and she was struggling financially. But she was a young woman who wanted to learn and was willing to grow. The fact that she was funny and joyful only strengthened that initial connection.

One Sunday several months after she'd started attending Oasis, Sherri came to me and said that her credit was so bad, because of previous credit-card debt and having once been evicted from her apartment, that she was struggling. Even though she had paid off her debts, she could not get a loan for a car, and she needed a vehicle for work. When she had tried to get the loan, they'd informed her, "No way will we give you a loan."

She asked if I would write a letter to help her get a loan. So I wrote a letter on Sherri's behalf. I didn't know if it would work, but I was willing to try. I'd never written a letter like that before, but in the letter I said that she was a faithful person, she had made a lot of good changes in her life, and I believed in her. I asked them to consider giving her a chance.

It worked! They reversed their decision and gave Sherri the loan. That did more in Sherri's heart than I ever dreamed.

After that she made a lot of changes. She learned responsibility, the value of having a good name or reputation, and the importance of moving forward no matter what.

And then she started getting acting work on TV and became one of the regulars on *Everybody Loves Raymond, Less Than Perfect,* and other shows. Holly and I would often tell Sherri, "Sometimes you have to do things scared even when you have fear. You still face the challenges that come along the way—you just do it scared. We believe in you. You can do it."

We've told many people that same thing through the years. Some people hear it and take the challenge; others do not. To be considered a mentor to Sherri was a great honor and encouragement. The value in a good mentoring situation is in both the mentor and the person following that encouragement. Being a mentor to someone can change the person's life in unanticipated ways. Being a mentor to someone makes you a dream-maker and opens doors for your own dreams. It motivates and inspires you to pursue the dream God has given you, and as I explained in the previous chapter on generosity, giving of yourself to others opens you to receive direction and blessing from God for your own dreams.

## Andrea's Story

Andrea loved to dance. One night while she was watching the Emmys, one of her friends pointed out a dancer he knew who was performing in the opening song. That recognition made Andrea want to have the same kind of fame, to have her face right there for everyone to see. So she moved to LA to become successful.

After living in LA for about three years and studying dance, she attended a fund-raiser to help support Steelo Vazquez, a professional dancer who'd had a brain aneurysm and who also happened to attend Oasis. Andrea had performed with Steelo and his wife, Penni, a few months earlier. At the fund-raiser, she heard about Steelo's faith in God, how God was healing him and restoring his movement, and how the doctors were surprised that he had survived at all. She was so moved by seeing Steelo come out in a wheelchair and stand that she wanted to know more about this God Steelo believed in. So she started to attend Oasis.

That's where she gave her life to Jesus. She learned that He was much more than the religious figure she had always thought He was. Jesus became a real and live presence in her life. And soon she realized that she could have a better life by serving God.

She volunteered to work with teenage girls at the church and watched as those girls realized that Jesus was all they needed to satisfy them in life. She got to see them break free from the pressures that young girls face growing up in our society. She helped them overcome problems, addictions, and heartbreaks.

As she continued to work with the girls, she discovered that they were changing her and her dreams. As she would audition or perform, she no longer felt comfortable doing certain routines or wearing immodest outfits. She realized that she had more to offer than just her body or her looks. "Showing skin or dancing seductively wasn't the thing I had to offer the world. I wanted to be the best example to young girls that I could be. I would ask myself, *Would I want these young girls seeing me do this?*" she told the Oasis congregation one Sunday.

When offered an audition for a music video, commercial, or show in Las

Vegas, she would ask herself, *Is this job going to make me wear something or do something I'm not comfortable with?*

Although she enjoyed pursuing her career, she decided to put aside her dance focus for a while. She still loved dancing and she still took and taught classes, but she wanted something more. No longer did being famous appeal to her as much as making a difference in the lives of the young women she worked with at church. #BeADreamMaker.

One day her agent called and told her that a choreographer she'd never worked with before wanted her for a job. The choreographer had said she felt a connection when looking at Andrea's photo and knew that Andrea was the right person. Andrea didn't even need to audition. "It turns out that this was one of the coolest opportunities I've had," she told our church. The job was dancing for Katy Perry's 2015 Grammy performance of "By the Grace of God."

> When we focus on God and the dream
> He has for our lives, there is no
> way to imagine the extent of what
> He can help us accomplish.

Andrea danced solo behind Katy as she sang. "Who could have planned that or made that happen? How could that happen with no effort on my part?" she told us. The job paid triple the normal pay rate, it was a huge audience, and she had done nothing to pursue it. In a way, the dream Andrea had that was sparked by watching the Emmys came true when she danced at the Grammys, but it happened because Andrea was doing what God wanted her to do.

"It was like God was saying to me, *You focus on trusting Me and helping*

*other people, and I can take care of your dancing career and other opportuni-*
*ties. See what I can do if you will trust Me."*

The most interesting aspect of her dancing at the Grammys was that she danced behind a scrim, a type of covering, so that only her silhouette was visible. "After all the attention I had put on myself about my appearance and looking 'good enough,' in that moment no one could see my face, but that was not really the issue." She smiled with confidence.

The Bible tells us that the humble are exalted, and that's what Andrea felt had happened. She was happy just serving and helping these girls and was faithful with what He had wanted her to do. "I want people who look at me not to see me but to see God's love. Just like when I was dancing as a silhou-ette, I'm a shadow of the light God shines on me."

The dream for her life now is about using her talents to reach people for Jesus, introduce them to a faith that is real, and inspire them to put their faith in Him.

Through Andrea's story we can see how the greatest Dream-Maker of all is on our side and wants us to do amazing things. When we focus on God and the dream He has for our lives, there is no way to imagine the extent of what He can help us accomplish.

### Helping One Somebody

Nanjing, China, is home to the Yangtze River Bridge, a location many people choose for committing suicide. It's painful to think of someone taking his or her own life, but many people struggle with difficult situations and don't know what to do.

When I first heard of the Yangtze River Bridge, it was because of Mr. Chen. News outlets like the *New York Times* and *GQ* have covered his story over the last ten years. Every weekend, Mr. Chen goes to the bridge to watch for people who may try to jump off. "It is very easy to recognize," he says. "A person walks without spirit."[5]

Suicide is the leading cause of death for Chinese citizens aged fifteen to thirty-four and the fifth leading cause of death for the entire population, according to a study by the Centers for Disease Control and Prevention.[6] Mr. Chen decided that was not okay with him, and he determined to make it his mission to help rescue those who feel that ending their lives is the only option.

"If I save one person," Mr. Chen says, "one is a lot."[7]

He takes the bus to the bridge and hands out pamphlets with his personal cell phone number as an emergency hotline. He talks people down, even tackles some, and then takes them to a restaurant to eat. He listens to their stories and tries to offer them hope to keep on living. Many have been rescued by his efforts.

As if this work alone weren't compelling enough, Mr. Chen said something that struck me: "I've saved lots of people, but one person alone isn't enough to do this work."[8]

Mr. Chen's story inspires me.

I think the things that make us mad, the issues that frustrate us, the pain we see in this world that we just can't stand all help to lead us to our dreams. For whatever reason, Mr. Chen couldn't stand the thought of someone losing hope and committing suicide. He didn't sit in his living room wishing someone else would do something, complaining that his government refused to do anything, or hoping every major news channel on the planet would tell his story. He just got up every weekend and volunteered to help, because one person matters to him. Every life counts. And that became his dream. Sometimes we discover our dreams when we step out to help others.

What would happen if we all got up and started helping just one somebody? What if we weren't so worried about who's watching or whether we'll get the credit but we just decided to help somebody? I wonder if more dreams would be fulfilled.

In moments when I snap out of the self-focused coma that occasionally captivates my attention, I begin to ask myself questions like, *What are the needs around me right now? What is it that makes me ask, "Why doesn't somebody do something about that?"* Then I have to ask, *Why don't I do something about it?*

God will bless a dream that is about making a difference in the lives of others. It's not always easy, and sometimes detours will hinder us, but if we can learn to overcome disappointment and setbacks, the God-dream will succeed.

An important key to unlocking our dreams is one that doesn't really have much at all to do with us. It has more to do with what we can do to help others unlock their dreams. Being a dream-maker is not just a calling God gives us; it is a privilege. As we go through life trying to realize our dreams, it is important to look beyond our own needs and desires to see how our journeys can benefit and lift up those around us. If there is only one message you remember, it should be this: No one makes it alone. We all need help getting there, whether it is through a message of encouragement, support to open doors, sacrifice to make a way, guidance when we get off course, or light in the darkness when we lose hope. God gives us all of this as He places a dream in our hearts and as He places people in our lives to help us realize it.

Our world needs you to shine. We need you to flourish. We need your compassion, your heart, and your contribution. We need *your* God-dreams to be fulfilled. Without what you bring to our world, life will be less than what is intended for all of us. It's part of my dream to release you so you can reach your dreams too.

We are called to reach out to humanity. We are assigned to help people live the lives that God has prepared for them. It's not about convenience or inconvenience. When we live in a way that helps others reach the dreams

God has prepared for them, we will discover a greater understanding of what our own lives and dreams are really all about.

|||

**DREAM LOCK:** Being self-focused prevents you from discovering what God may be trying to teach you through helping others.

**DREAM KEY:** When you help others reach their dreams, you get another step closer to your dream and discovering what it is all about.

**SCRIPTURE KEY:** Don't be selfish; don't try to impress others. Be humble, thinking of others as better than yourselves. Don't look out only for your own interests, but take an interest in others, too. (Philippians 2:3–4, NLT)

# When the Heavens Open

> Deep into that darkness peering, long I stood there, wondering, fearing, / Doubting, dreaming dreams no mortal ever dared to dream before.
>
> —EDGAR ALLAN POE, "THE RAVEN"

Have you ever had the feeling that heaven's doors were shut tight and there was no way you could open them? I've been through times like that when I would pray and it seemed as if God wasn't listening. It can feel defeating.

You may be trying to reach your dreams and feel stuck. The circumstances seem overwhelming, and you aren't sure if you're on the right track, if you're going to succeed. Other questions might make you doubt your dream. It seems only to make things worse when you feel as if God isn't working on your behalf or even listening to your prayers.

These are the times you need to remind yourself that God hasn't forgotten you or your dreams. He continues to work in your life. Just because you don't see signs of your dream progressing doesn't mean that God isn't involved.

The Bible tells a story about the prophet Elisha and his servant who were in the Israelite town of Dothan. They found themselves surrounded by an enemy army. It didn't look promising for their survival. Elisha's companion was understandably afraid. Elisha told him not to worry because "those who are with us are more than those who are with them." Elisha prayed for God to open his servant's eyes. Then the invisible veil that hid God's unimaginable workings from the servant's limited human vision was pulled back like a curtain hanging in the universe to reveal heaven's support: an angel army.[1]

We experience an open heaven when our spiritual eyes are opened and we realize that God *is* on our side. Right now. In this situation. When the heavens open we get a glimpse of God's purpose, the gifts He's given us, and the protection He brings.

Knowing that you have an army of angels working with you changes everything. God is telling you, *I am with you, I got this, so don't think you are defeated.* You will unlock your dreams when you discover that there is an open heaven . . . right where you are. Right now.

In chapter 2 we talked about embracing our extraordinary ordinary life, that the first key to unlocking our dreams is pursuing extraordinariness in the way God has designed and planned for us. That's the kind of life of dreams I want to have. Do you?

## Seeing Jesus in Your Story
## Unlocks the Extraordinary

When Jesus walked into a room, miracles started to happen. Blind eyes would see and people who were crippled would get up and walk. When Jesus entered the story, people found hope and they felt loved. Forgiveness was granted, storms became peaceful, and the powers of darkness were driven out when Jesus stepped onto the scene.

In 1977, an art-restoration specialist named Pinin Barcilon was asked to lead the team working on restoring Leonardo da Vinci's famous work *The Last Supper,* one of the most well-known paintings of all time. Barcilon never imagined the difficulties she would face, or the interesting discoveries that would be revealed, in the twenty-three years it would take to complete the job. Amateurs had painted over da Vinci's work many times, distorting its images, covering over details they didn't understand, and filling in gaps with their own interpretations. On a good day, she would uncover a postage stamp–sized portion of the original image.

Over the years, the dingy shadows vanished and a well-lit banquet room emerged. Peter's beard no longer had the awkward additions that came from retouchings, and his "nose job" was corrected to a slimmer, more original version. Matthew's black dye job was reversed and he was returned his original blond. She gave Thomas his left hand, and Andrew no longer looked like he was brooding, but astonished, as da Vinci intended.

The part of the restoration project that was the most inspiring to me was how Jesus's face glowed with new light after the dull reworkings had been removed.[2]

That's what happened to me. My personal restoration project began when Jesus became real to me and I saw Him with new light. When the dullness that had been painted over Jesus was removed, I realized that heaven had opened over my life. Jesus became the focus.

We get bogged down by the interpretations that others paint over our dreams. We don't believe that God is really working in our lives, so we let discouragement tarnish our confidence in the dream He gave us. Our faith grows dull. Shadows begin to cover the brilliance that our dreams once had. Without our realizing it, the vibrancy of our faith wanes and we get accustomed to a reduced rendition of the King of kings.

When we invite Jesus into our story, the heavens are opened and our view of Him becomes more vivid. Jesus gets clearer the more we pursue Him. He emerges, Prince of Peace, Healer, Miracle Worker, Shepherd, and Friend.

A genuine faith is one that guides us and brings strength to our lives. We know we will face situations that do not make sense and that we don't understand. We need to discover a faith that transcends circumstances.

Jesus told us that some mountains can be cast into the sea.[3] I believe that some mountains are to be climbed by the strength He gives us. Either way it requires faith that comes from a direct connection with Jesus Himself.

Trusting Jesus is the focus of our lives: We trust that where Jesus is leading us is the best place we could go. Trusting that He knows how we'll get there removes anxiety from our lives. Trusting in God's promises for us will unlock heaven's power to lead us toward our dream.

When we see through the eyes of faith what *could be,* our eyes begin to see life differently. We live as if we, like Elisha's servant, have seen what's behind the veil. Trusting God will remind us of the song that He put in our hearts.

### Relying on God's Grace
### Unlocks Extraordinary Dreams

It is incredible to realize that God knows about our weaknesses and our failures and that He *still* loves us. Jesus knew about them before He died for us and made the sacrifice anyway: "For God so loved the world that he gave his one and only Son . . ."[4]

We can't earn that kind of love. We don't deserve this magnitude of love. The depth of His love for us requires that we share it with others.

When Jesus was baptized, the heavens opened for Him. He heard His Father's voice come from the heavens. God said, "This is my Son, whom I love; with him I am well pleased."[5] This is what Jesus heard before He went on to live the most impactful three years of anyone who has ever lived.

I'm convinced that the greatest thing you could ever hear is the voice of your heavenly Father speaking to your heart: *I love you. You are one I've chosen. I'm pleased with you. I am with you.* Those words would shape anyone's life, whether this declaration came as a shout from the heavens or a whisper into the core of who you are. Those words of heaven's affirmation fill you with the grace to be able to help the people you encounter in the travels of your extraordinary life. Knowing His grace toward you allows you to find the extraordinary in other people's lives as well.

## Refusing to Give Up
## Unlocks Extraordinary Dreams

I love horses. They are amazing and majestic animals. For years, horseback riding on the hundreds of miles of trails in LA County was my way to escape the city in order to decompress. I agree with the quote attributed to Ronald Reagan: "There's something about the outside of a horse that is good for the inside of a man." Riding a horse has been one way for me to reenergize and refocus to pursue my dreams.

I've faced many challenges in which I felt I didn't have the strength to go on, but through God's strength, I've found a way to continue. I may not be the most talented or the most powerful, but when I've lacked other resources, I have had perseverance. Dreams need our commitment.

When I get weary or wonder if God is going to help me, I think about how God described the power of a horse ready for battle:

It paws fiercely, rejoicing in its strength,
    and charges into the fray.
It laughs at fear, afraid of nothing;
    it does not shy away from the sword.
The quiver rattles against its side,
    along with the flashing spear and lance.
In frenzied excitement it eats up the ground;
    it cannot stand still when the trumpet sounds.[6]

God says, "I give the horse his majestic strength, and I will give *you* the strength you need. Just follow Me." Don't give up. Keep going, even when everything inside you wants to quit. The journey to realizing your dreams will not be easy, and it may be long and exhausting, but you can be assured that whether it is full of hurdles, long and winding, or fearful and treacherous, you will not travel that road alone.

### Jesus, the Hope of Heaven, Unlocks Extraordinary Dreams

All dreamers will find themselves in desperate situations—broken hearts, shattered dreams, discontent, and shaken to the core. The subsequent results can be destructive or they can be extraordinary.

There is a story in the gospel of Mark about a woman who lived in a horrible situation.[7] She had been sick and bleeding for twelve years, which, in her world, was a cause for shame. Many people in her community shunned her. She was considered unclean. Even to touch her would have been a serious offense in that culture.

The woman had spent a lot of money—all she had—on doctors and their remedies. Nothing worked and she had slowly lost hope. Her dreams had faded and her emotions were raw.

At times I've felt like I've tried everything to fix a relationship problem, an emotional battle, or a financial crisis I've faced, yet nothing made it better. In fact, often it grew worse, in spite of or maybe because of my efforts. Have you ever felt as though you've tried everything—read the books, got the counseling, lost the weight—but instead of getting better, you found yourself at the end of your rope?

When this woman had heard about Jesus and that He healed people, a flickering light of hope stirred deep inside her. She wanted to hear more. "She kept saying, If I only touch His garments, I shall be restored to health."[8] Somehow, despite her failed attempts to find healing, despite remaining stuck in her circumstances, she believed Jesus held the key to her healing.

What does the voice coming from your own heart say? Is it an accusation? A judgment? Maybe it proclaims, *You're done! Your dreams are finished!* Or perhaps you hear a voice of courage say above the inner noise, *I'm going to try again. I've got one more try in me.*

The faith of the woman caught Jesus's attention. You might think, *I don't have much faith. I'm too wounded to have faith.* But faith is not always what we think it is. Sometimes our faith is expressed in the things that don't register to mere mortals. The woman showed up and reached out. That was it. And Jesus said, "Wow! Your faith has healed you."

There's something about that name: Jesus, Yeshua, the name above every name! Jesus, the Messiah: His name brings hope to those who hear it. When you start to lose hope in ever realizing your dreams, call out in the name of Jesus, and find out that His name will open the heavens to you; you will find the hope you need.

A genuine encounter with Jesus Christ changes everyone, no matter who you are or what you've been through. Jesus redefines us as people and redefines our futures. If we can allow heaven to infiltrate the secret places of our hearts, the Holy Spirit has power to impart to us.

If you have a dream that's alive in you, if you still have the slightest hope and imagine that maybe, just maybe, Jesus is coming your way, and if you desire to have enough faith to make a change, reach out to Him, because you qualify.

Faith involves reaching forward into the things you do not yet have so you can bring them into your present.

The woman who pursued healing from Jesus went behind Him in the crowd and touched the corner of His garment. It seems like such a small gesture. It was more than a gesture; it was an act of faith. An enemy of faith is fear, but she pushed through it. An enemy of faith is shame, but she stood in opposition to the voice of darkness shouting accusations about her value.

She could have wondered, *What if I reach out and once again, instead of getting better, nothing happens, or I get worse? Do I dare reach out to Jesus? Can I trust another person?* Instead she made the best decision of her life. She reached out to Jesus.

> Twenty years from now you will be more disappointed by the things you didn't do than by the ones you did do. So throw off the bowlines. Sail away from the safe harbor. Catch the trade winds in your sails. Explore. Dream. Discover.
>
> —H. Jackson Brown Jr.'s mother, *P.S. I Love You*

Have you been caught in the chains of despair? Does your past infiltrate your present so that you don't know how to move forward with your dream? It's not that you haven't tried. You've made the lifestyle changes, sought advice from friends or professionals, and given it all your focus and effort, but instead of getting better, things keep getting worse. Doubts creep into your heart, and insecurities develop and surface. You're doing the best you can, but it just doesn't seem enough.

Jesus revives dead things. Jesus resurrects dead dreams. When we get to the end of our efforts and it's still not enough, we can trust that Jesus is enough. We can stop placing all our hope and energy in things that don't produce what we desire and place our hope in Him.

Then Jesus will say to us, "Your faith has healed you."[9]

I imagine their surprise when He asked His disciples, "Who touched me?"[10]

"Umm, Jesus, this is a large crowd. Lots of people touched you."

Her faith touched Him. Sometimes when we feel like we don't have anything at all, we have all we need: faith. Simply believing in Jesus and reaching forward into the things we do not yet have is the faith that allows us to see what could be, what must be.

In a genuine encounter with Jesus, He qualifies the unqualified. He gives us new vision. He revives the dreams He has put in our hearts. Failures become opportunities for new beginnings. Stagnant seasons of life find momentum. The pain of the past leads to purpose.

The woman risked everything, literally, to touch Jesus. She pressed through the shame of every failed attempt at healing, the shame of being unclean for twelve years, to touch Jesus. She used her faith to fight her fear of touching a rabbi in a crowd of men in a society that oppressed women.

And Jesus healed her. He healed her! Jesus did what an ordinary man could not do. He validated her faith. He treated her in a way that transcended her circumstances. He freed her. He empowered her. Publicly.

Is there an area of your life you've given up on? You can trust Jesus to help you try again. I can tell you, it's worth it. Give Jesus a chance. You have one more try in you. This time try it with Jesus—and let heaven open itself to you.

## Julian's Story

I want to tell you why I do what I do, why I continue to be a pastor in a local church. It's because there might just be a young man with a dream in his heart who is sitting in the church audience and is thinking about giving up. I'm trying to reach that guy. There is a chance that as I'm speaking, heaven opens up to his life.

There might just be a young woman who has had an unimpressive start in life and needs hope. There is a strong possibility that while I'm speaking, heaven just may open over her life.

I wasted my twenties, an important time of life. I did little of significance at that age. The lack of significance in my twenties became the significance of my twenties. It hit me after I missed it. In my thirties and forties I realized I had wasted that precious time. I think that God has redeemed some of that lost time by allowing me to reach young adults and help them understand the impact of their decisions.

When Julian was nineteen years old, he saw his mother die. She began having shortness of breath and feeling faint. He and his twin brother, Jason, thought she was having a stroke so they called 911. The paramedics arrived, but they couldn't save her. The last words he heard his mother say were "Help me, Jesus."

Complicating the sadness of his mother's death was the reality that he'd had a difficult relationship with her. She hadn't received much love or affirmation as a young girl, so she didn't know how to give love to her kids. Julian doesn't remember his mom ever saying she loved him.

"I don't remember her hugging me," Julian told me. "I don't think it was because she didn't want to; she didn't know how. She expressed her hurt and anger by being verbally abusive to me and my brother, so I grew up hating my mom."

He spent his early adulthood pursuing things that made him feel good, at least temporarily. But the bitterness from his childhood kept surfacing, and he started struggling with depression and smoking marijuana. When he was thirty-one, he heard the Holy Spirit say to him, *I'm calling you to help young people.*

"Okay, Jesus, I'll do it," he said. He was willing, but he did not know how.

One night a few months later, a friend invited him to a men's small group. Julian said, "I can't go. I've been smoking pot and I'm a little high."

"Don't worry, you will be welcomed," his friend reassured him. "It will be good for you to go."

Julian decided that he could fake it, so he went with his friend to the group. He had a great time there. After the meeting was over, one of the men took Julian aside and asked him privately, "Are you high?" Julian admitted that he was, and he was surprised when the man encouraged him to continue going to the group so Julian could find the help he needed.

He went a couple of times and then missed one of the meetings a couple of weeks later because he was high. His friend contacted him again and said, "Keep coming to our meetings. Even if you are high, don't miss them."

One Saturday morning, after a men's gathering, I saw Julian and asked if he had been coming to Oasis or if he was a new attender. He told me he had been coming to Oasis and attending another church too but wasn't sure where he should go.

Julian asked me, "How should I decide which church to go to? I haven't grown in my faith a whole lot at the other church, and I like Oasis, but I'm not sure what I should do."

"I'm going to give you a challenge," I told him. "Give Oasis one year. Come to church regularly, go all in, get involved in serving in some area in the church, go to a Connect group, and see what happens to you. If, after one year, you aren't more clear about God's purpose for your life, more knowledgeable of God's Word, more familiar with the presence of God, have good friends, and feel stronger in your faith than ever, then you should leave Oasis and find another church that has a better impact."

Julian took the challenge and has been at Oasis ever since.

He got involved with serving in youth ministry. The calling from God that he'd heard years earlier got stronger. He forgave his mom and found healing from those hurts in his heart. He's now one of the pastors at Oasis.

"I can say I truly love my mom now," Julian tells people.

He said to me, "My dream is to help other people's dreams come to pass. Most of the things that I have done didn't really fulfill me. What satisfies me is to help other people reach their dreams. I want to help unlock someone else's dream. I want to lead people to Jesus."

Julian chose to try again with Jesus. And so can you.

It's time to dream again. It's time to shake off the chains of regret and get new vision for your life. Sing like you hear the music of heaven.

## Break Through to Your Dreams

When things go wrong, our faith will help us to find a way. Many people think we are defined by our worst day or our worst decision, but we are not! We are defined by the way we love and the actions we take. We are defined by our trust in God.

Proverbs reminds us to "trust in the LORD with all your heart; do not depend on your own understanding. Seek his will in all you do, and he will show you which path to take."[11] People need to know that God qualifies the called, not calls the qualified. If the validity of my faith is defined only by successes and blessings, my faith will one day be shipwrecked. I want a faith that is still strong even if the circumstances don't turn out the way I thought they would.

When we think of reaching the God-dreams for our lives, living an extraordinary life, or building a legacy, it is normal to want grand results, so we tend to look for grand opportunities. But they are hidden in the needs right in front of us. We must recognize there is something amazing going on *right in front of us.* There is an open heaven.

You might feel like you are going through a fight right now. You are struggling because you feel that you are not what you used to be; there is a spark missing in your life. You believe you are off your game, and you are out of your rhythm. It's time to turn your focus toward heaven.

If you open yourself to God and don't allow hurts to define you, God will do miracles in your life and in the lives of people around you. God can empower anyone who will risk enough to believe Him.

The path to reaching our dreams is full of obstacles. We are not guaranteed a smooth run, even if what we desire is actually what God wants for us—the dreams He put in our hearts. In the face of difficulties and hopeless-ness, we have access to the kind of strength we cannot orchestrate ourselves, and in that we have every resource we will ever need to make our dreams a reality.

|||

**DREAM LOCK:** When you feel far from God, you lose the confidence you need to reach your God-dream.

**DREAM KEY:** You can live a life with real, genuine faith. Turn your focus toward heaven, and discover what God can do in you and through you.

**SCRIPTURE KEY:** Look! I stand at the door and knock. If you hear my voice and open the door, I will come in. (Revelation 3:20, NLT)

# If This Were My Last Week on Earth

> Always go to other people's funerals, otherwise they won't go to yours.
>
> —YOGI BERRA

If this were my last week on Earth, first of all, I'd like to have a little more warning. You know, like a pink slip or a yellow notice. Maybe just a whispered *I wouldn't plan too heavily on going to that concert next month.*

I think it's because I wish I were more prepared. I am living my dream life, but when it comes to my last week on Earth, I don't think the feeling of *I wish I were more prepared* is going to go away. It seems like there is always more I'd like to do.

Not long before the apostle Paul died, he put some of his final thoughts in a letter to Timothy: "I'm about to die, my life an offering on God's altar. This is the only race worth running. I've run hard right to the finish, believed all the way. All that's left now is the shouting—God's applause!"[1]

We all know we are going to have a "last week"; we just aren't clear on the exact date of that week.

Randy Pausch wrote the *New York Times* best-selling book *The Last Lecture.* It was born out of a lecture Pausch gave at Carnegie Mellon University in September 2007, titled "Really Achieving Your Childhood Dreams." This talk was modeled after an ongoing series of lectures where top academics were asked to think deeply about what matters to them and then give a hypothetical final talk, sort of like the wisdom you would try to impart to the world if you knew it was your last chance.

A month before giving the lecture, Pausch received a prognosis that the pancreatic cancer he had been diagnosed with a year earlier was terminal. During the lecture Pausch was upbeat and humorous, shrugging off the pity often given to those diagnosed with terminal illnesses. He talked about his childhood dreams and said, "Inspiration and the permission to dream are huge."

One of the most meaningful points he made came at the very end, when he stated, "It's not about how to achieve your dreams. It's about how to lead your life."[2]

I want to finish strong. I want to have made the best of what time God has given me. For me, a major part of finishing strong is not just accomplishing meaningful things but leaving a legacy of who I am with those I love. I have this feeling that if I died suddenly, there would be too much that died with me—thoughts I wanted to express, lessons I wanted to pass on, and advice I wanted to give.

If this were my last week, this is what I'd say to you, my fellow dreamer, about living and reaching your dreams.

## 1. Make Time to Laugh

An urban legend says children laugh about four hundred times per day, but by the time we are adults we barely laugh at all; some estimate only ten to fifteen times per day.[3]

I don't know who is watching all day and counting how many times we laugh as adults, but I know I need to laugh more. A lot more. I know this because when I have a really good laugh, I think, *It feels so good to laugh. I need to do that more often.*

Norman Cousins famously chronicled the effects of his self-prescribed "laughing cure" in *Anatomy of an Illness: As Perceived by the Patient*. Cousins, who suffered from inflammatory arthritis, claimed that ten minutes of hearty guffawing while watching Marx Brothers movies allowed him to sleep for two hours without pain and that both his inflammation and pain were significantly reduced.[4] His views resulted in this philosophy: "Death is not the greatest loss in life. The greatest loss is what dies inside us while we live."

I believe if we don't intentionally find times to laugh or create the opportunities for having fun, we may always be too busy.

Hang out with friends who make you laugh. Tell funny stories. Reminisce about joyful moments. Watch movies that are comedies. Listen to a good comedian perform.

My comedian friend Michael Jr. said one of his goals is to "make laughter common in uncommon places." I like this idea. Laughter is a sign of hope. Michael Jr. believes that God gets pleasure when we laugh.

Laughter is the best sound in the world. Indulge in a sense of humor.

## 2. Occasionally You Gotta Dance Like No One Is Watching

When I was in high school and college I really liked to dance. In my twenties I used to dance with my friends at parties. Somewhere along the way, I lost my dance. Really. I danced at my wedding, I've danced at a couple of events, but over time I realized that at some point I just enjoyed watching people dance.

I recruited some dancers in our church to start a dance team, not just to add creativity to a special song in our gatherings, but because people who *can* dance can cause others to experience some of the freedom the dancers feel when they are dancing.

If you have rhythm issues, the good news is that "dance like no one is watching" is a metaphor for celebrating, playing, and carving out moments to experience joy.

> *We dance for laughter, we dance for tears,*
> *we dance for madness, we dance for fears,*
> *we dance for hopes, we dance for screams,*
> *we are the dancers, we create the dreams.*
>
> —Albert Einstein

A few years ago, I decided to rediscover "my dance." So Holly and I took ballroom-dancing classes. She picked up everything quickly, and I looked like I wasn't having any fun because I was looking down and counting, "One, two, three, four. One, two, three, four."

Apparently I looked like I was trying to solve a higher math problem or figure out how to end world hunger while simultaneously moving my feet.

"Philip, smile. This is fun," the instructor said. "You are supposed to be enjoying it!"

"Okay," I said as I concentrated on my next steps. "One, two, three, four, *smile*. One, two, three, four, *smile*."

Finally the instructor said, "Let me give a couple of pointers to you both. Holly, you have to stop leading. He is supposed to lead." (An appropriate metaphor for our relationship.)

Holly added, "If you don't lead, I'm going to."

"No, you can't do that," the instructor asserted.

"Thank you!" I whispered. "I've been trying to say that for years."

"Philip, you are supposed to lead. Be confident. If you are uncertain, she is uncertain. Don't take such big steps, don't look down at your feet, stand up straight, be confident, and feel it."

"Can I write this down?"

"You don't need to. You will just feel it," the instructor said. He had no idea whom he was dealing with.

"Can I have an Advil? Or a glass of wine? Or both?"

"And don't forget to smile," he added. "You are supposed to be having fun."

"Oh. Okay. Thanks for adding that last part. *Fun.* Let me write that down."

We eventually got better. A little. "We" mostly means Holly.

Dance when you are happy. Dance when you are struggling. Dance when you are hurting. Dance when you need to celebrate. It's worth it. There comes a time when we all need to see what our lives look like from the dance floor.

My point is, dance and don't hold back.

### 3. Continually Improve Your Serve

Help someone reach his or her goals or dreams. Try helping someone and not getting credit for it. Learn to recognize when you are doing *just enough,* then do a little more.

Look for times to say to others, "Do you need anything?" This practice keeps us thinking of others and being aware of the needs around us. It keeps an important focus in our lives. Jesus said, "Whoever wants to become great among you must be your servant."[5]

A few years ago I became a sort of big brother to Shemar, a boy who was being raised by a single mom in our church. I do have a lot on my plate, but I felt that whisper that comes up inside me occasionally. *I could be an example not just to Shemar but to inspire other men who don't realize the impact they could have on a young man's life.*

I realized that time spent with a man who will encourage him is crucial for a young boy, and while I can't do this for many kids, I can do it for him.

When I said yes to Shemar, I remembered hearing pastor Andy Stanley once say, "Do for one what you wish you could do for everyone."[6]

One of our first outings was to Universal Studios. We were having a great time together. While we waited in one of the long lines for a ride, Shemar held my hand and said, "I bet people looking at us think you're my dad."

I thought about this for a moment, mentally noting that I'm Caucasian and Shemar is African American. "You might be right," I said smiling. "They probably do think that."

We have been spending time together for about five years now. We just do simple stuff—run errands together, go to Starbucks, or have lunch. I call him to see how he's doing, and he texts me sometimes. He's outgoing and acts like he's never met a stranger. He will say overtly friendly things to random people we meet, but people always seem to open up to him. There's something special about him.

Shemar and I go to Dodgers and Lakers games together, or we go to the movies. I've enrolled him at summer camps and to play basketball and baseball, trying to encourage him in his enjoyment of sports. I used to pay him a couple of dollars to read a book and then discuss it with me. He excelled at this.

> As we lose ourselves in the service of others, we discover our own lives and our own happiness.
>
> —Dieter F. Uchtdorf

Shemar is a great kid. He's good in school. He's smart. He's compassionate. He has always talked like he was five years older than his actual age. He remembers *everything*. (Which makes us a good team.)

His mom's name is Brandy. A fourteen-year-old girl was giving birth at the hospital where Brandy's mom worked as a nurse and was going to give up the baby to social services. Brandy and her mom decided they would adopt him.

Brandy's mom passed away with cancer a few months later, and Brandy decided at twenty-one years old that she would raise this boy. She became his mom by choice. Brandy was an exceptional woman who made the decision of a lifetime with an intentional act of love and self-sacrifice.

I'm a better person because of having Shemar and Brandy in my life. If you look around, you might find that you actually do have the time to make a difference in someone's life. You could be the positive role model that you wish you'd had. And if you did have a great role model, you could make that same positive impact in someone else's life.

If you're fortunate like me, you might find someone like Shemar and discover your investment in their life might have as much impact on you as it does on them.

## 4. Love Like You've Never Been Hurt

This one is a tough one. "Love like you've never been hurt" means that even after heartbreaks or disappointments, we have to find our way back to loving in a way that is pure and without fear of our love being rejected. Rediscover how to trust but with more discretion.

We are created to love and be loved. When we aren't experiencing both of those, we don't function well. Everyone is going to get hurt sometime in life. Getting hurt is part of life. Being disappointed in someone you love is inevitable. But if you live trying to protect yourself from hurts, you will never love fully. If we can survive the hurts and not show the pain in our attitude, we are moving in the right direction.

I hate feeling the pain that has been caused by those I've loved and trusted. But if I could do it all again, I would, because I'd rather live a life that includes the moments that I loved fully and was hurt than to live in a way that protects me from relational pain but also keeps me from being loved. Dream without fear, and love without limits.

## 5. Live Like You're Leaving a Legacy

Tug McGraw was a great pitcher in the major leagues. He won two World Series with the New York Mets and was one of the best closing pitchers in Philadelphia Phillies history. McGraw was a team cheerleader; he inspired others to keep going. He's the guy who started the popular phrase of his day "You gotta believe!"

After his career in baseball, he became a game announcer for television. He might still be in broadcasting today if it hadn't been for the sudden change in his health in 2003. By the time the doctors discovered the illness, they told Tug, who was fifty-nine years old, that he had three weeks to live.

Three weeks! But he lived for nine months. He spent that nine months investing in his family in a way he had not before. He poured his energy into building a legacy dedicated to curing the disease he was fighting and to reconciling with a part of his past he'd ignored.

He had a wife and kids, but he also had another son who was born before he met and married his wife. He had ignored his estranged son for years. The mother of that boy didn't tell her son about his famous baseball father, in part because she wanted to move past that particular part of her life too.

But this young boy, Tim, one day found his birth certificate and made the shocking discovery that his favorite baseball player, Tug McGraw, was also his father. Later that boy changed his name from Tim Trimble to Tim McGraw.

When he was a teenager, Tim met Tug, but there were no warm feelings, no immediate connection, and apparently no future to their relationship.

Once more, now as an adult, Tim tried to connect with his dad. This time, the connection took. Father and son, as strange as it must have seemed to them, became close.

Tim went on to become the famous country-music singer, writer, and actor. He has appeared in such movies as *The Blind Side* and *Friday Night Lights*. So far ten of his albums have reached number one on the charts, and twenty-five of his songs have reached number one. He has won three Grammys, and his Soul2Soul tour is one of the top-five grossing tours among all genres of music.

When the news came that his dad's time was running out, the two became closer still. In the end, Tug McGraw died at his once-estranged son's home in Nashville.

In 2004 Tim McGraw's song "Live Like You Were Dying" stayed on top of the charts for ten weeks, breaking a record that had stood for thirty years. The song was about a man who got the news that he was dying, a man who made new decisions about how he would live with the time he had left. Tim sang about going skydiving and mountain climbing. The lyrics speak of his own great exchange: "And I loved deeper . . . and gave forgiveness I'd been denying." He sang of the revelation he gained by knowing his time was quickly coming to an end. He added that he became the kind of a friend that friends would like to have.[7]

Why wait until our lives are almost over to have the journey of a lifetime? Tim ended the chorus of the song with the hope that others would get the chance to live like they were dying.

The truth is we are all running out of time. The opportunity to leave the legacy we want to leave is one day shorter than it was yesterday. Maybe we shouldn't actually live like we are dying but live like we understand what life and legacy are all about. It will take more than one week to leave the impact of a life full of love.

Many people start to think about their legacies when they hit fifty. We stop thinking only of achievements, we stop thinking about being a success and instead start thinking about living lives of significance, to leave positive impacts on the lives of those around us. Whatever your age, now is the time to live like you're leaving a legacy . . . because you are.

## 6. Pray Like God Is Actually on Your Side

Prayer works! Faith moves mountains. Prayer is God's idea. When we pray and really believe God hears us right then, we discover the power of prayer. It's the idea that if you're going to pray for rain, you should carry an umbrella with you.

Having this kind of confidence in prayer will change the quality of your life and your dreams. Our free access to God is one of the greatest benefits of our faith. Jesus paid the way so we could go directly to our Father with our needs.

I have specific times in my day for undistracted prayer, but I also pray on the go. You can't thrive on the "pray as you go" kind of prayers, but they can be powerful. Smith Wigglesworth once stated, "I don't often spend more than half an hour in prayer at one time, but I never go more than half an hour without praying."

I like that strategy.

Many times we have to pray when we least feel like it. It's not our ability to say great prayers that matters so much as our effort to connect with God personally and invite Him into our circumstances. Prayer changes circumstances, it changes people, and it changes us.

If we did an honest evaluation of our prayer lives, I think we would recognize that a large percentage of our prayers are aimed at solving problems. Most of us pray that God will keep us out of troubles and storms. We ask God to help us steer clear of trials, awkward situations with people, and traffic on the California freeway, Interstate 405. However, a lot of the time the great impact of our prayers is how they prepare us for the situations we face as well as the changes brought to specific needs we pray for.

God is listening. Go ahead and talk to Him.

## 7. Resist Worrying About "Things"

A friend told me that his grandparents were among the people who had purchased tickets to go on the maiden voyage of the *Titanic*. They were so excited for this dream adventure. They sacrificed and saved their precious money to take this trip of a lifetime. But this couple struggled to overcome delays in their travel to the dock, and they arrived so late that they could only watch, heartbroken, as their dreams sailed off into the distance.

We know how that story ends. The ship sank and more than fifteen hundred people died. It was not an end for my friend's grandparents, though. Missing the boat was actually an opportunity for them to continue living, continue pursuing their dreams, only now they understood in a deeper way that their lives were gifts.

I worry about the details too much. It's usually the missed details that wreck a special moment. But after trying so hard to do it all *right*, I find myself worn out from all the *trying*. Dreams can come true because of hard work, but working too hard and worrying about getting everything just right can become a weight that we cannot carry.

God has a way, which we can never fully anticipate, of working things out. There are moments when we need to just leave the details to God. Because sometimes those details save our lives and our dreams, as happened for the couple who missed boarding the *Titanic*. I often have to remind myself that God says, "My thoughts are nothing like your thoughts. . . . And my ways are far beyond anything you could imagine."[8]

### Final Thoughts

If I could do all it again, I would. I imagine that I would do it better the second time around, but that's probably not true. Since it's not possible anyway, I want to take the best of what I have and make this one life full of dreaming, becoming, and lifting up others along the way.

We have an incredible opportunity to do something extraordinary because God designed us with a special and unique purpose in mind. He has given us each a dream. In our journey we need to discover what that dream is and then align our efforts with God's guidance to attain what He wants us to accomplish.

The purpose of this book is to help you discover the keys that unlock your dreams and remove the barriers that stand in the way of having the full life God has planned for you. It is to help you realize that our world needs you to shine. We need you to flourish. We need your compassion, your heart, and your contribution. Without what you bring to our world, life will be less than what is intended for all of us.

Life is going to involve detours, roadblocks, and delays, but if you keep moving forward, learning what you can each step of the way, you will get there, and you will arrive fully prepared for the dream that awaits.

Enjoy the journey, encourage people you encounter along the way in their own dreams, allow God to lead, and open yourself up to the possibilities.

You have a dream in your heart.

Unlock it.

|||

**DREAM LOCKS:** Life's challenges and problems can cause you to take your eyes off your true priorities, bogging you down in the urgent, never getting back to the important.

**DREAM KEY:** Learning to live with "what really matters" as your compass and finding your way out of survival mode will keep you moving toward your dream.

**SCRIPTURE KEY:** Be careful how you live. Don't live like fools, but like those who are wise. Make the most of every opportunity in these evil days. Don't act thoughtlessly, but understand what the Lord wants you to do. (Ephesians 5:15–17, NLT)

# Dream-Builder
# Discussion Questions

**Chapter 1: Interpreting Your Dreams**

1. What dreams do you have? What has kept you from pursuing those dreams?

2. There are also God-dreams, those dreams that God has placed inside you that are key to the greatest fulfillment you could have. What is your God-dream? What keeps you from pursuing it with abandon?

**Chapter 2: Your Extraordinary, Ordinary Life**

1. Are you missing great opportunities around you right now because you are looking for something different to happen? While you anticipate something else, what could you be missing that is right in front of you?

2. Have you allowed your current life season to become dull in your own mind? How can you create a fresh way to look at your work, your goal, or your dream? In what ways can you keep your eyes open today to pursue the extraordinary in the ordinary moments?

**Chapter 3: The Great Exchange**

1. Are you being unrealistic about how long your dream could take? Are you honestly ready to work on everything that you need to?

2. Is there anything that you're unwilling to exchange, even if it means jeopardizing your dream?

**Chapter 4: Distractions, Divine Interruptions, and Defining Moments**

1. Has there been an experience in your life that you now think could have been a divine interruption you should have followed? Is there

something you've seen that really moves you and could be a divine interruption?

2. Have you gotten off track from an important dream because you were distracted by another opportunity? The next time that occurs, how should you respond?

### Chapter 5: If You Build It, He Will Come

1. Are you really willing to take a big risk, a leap of faith toward something, which if it works out could be a game changer in your life?

2. Is there something you're letting slip away that you might one day look back at and wonder, *Why didn't I give it a try?*

### Chapter 6: Finding Your Way in a Desert

1. In the times when you've wanted to quit, what has helped you to keep going and to persevere?

2. Whom could you look to as a mentor or advisor who can help you in your journey?

### Chapter 7: Dream Thieves

1. What have you allowed to steal your dreams? In what ways can you stop these thieves?

2. How do you develop faith that transcends circumstances?

### Chapter 8: Choosing Friends

1. Who are your most important friends? Do they add to your efforts to reach your dream? In what ways? Do you support them in their dreams?

2. Who has been a friend and told you things you needed to hear even though it was difficult to hear at first?

### Chapter 9: The Unwelcome Crisis

1. What can you do to develop a faith that is greater than your circumstances?
2. What scriptures can you hold on to that will bring you strength?

### Chapter 10: Betrayal's Burden

1. Have you experienced a betrayal that you have left buried and refused to resolve?
2. In what ways have you allowed your bitterness toward that person to short-circuit your dream?

### Chapter 11: I'll Have What They're Having

1. What has caused you to feel discontent? What can you do about it? Can you change the situation, or do you need to change your view of it?
2. What ideas do you have to consistently turn your attitude from discontent to gratitude?

### Chapter 12: The Generosity Factor

1. Who has been generous to you? How did their generosity impact you?
2. Who can use some help? In what ways can you be the generous person in their story?

### Chapter 13: Being a Dream-Maker

1. Is there someone who helped you reach one of your dreams? How did that person become a dream-maker to you?
2. How can you help others reach their dreams? Is there someone you can help take another step toward his or her dream?

### Chapter 14: When the Heavens Open

1. What mountains of difficulty have you faced that you need help from God to get over?
2. If you knew Jesus was with you through all the difficulties, how would that glimpse of an "open heaven" redefine your future?

### Chapter 15: If This Were My Last Week on Earth

1. If you knew you had one year left, what would you change about how you spend your time and where you put your focus?
2. What is one relationship you would like to invest more time in because of that person's importance to you?

# Acknowledgments

Every dream reached involves a dream team of people who were part of the journey. No dream is reached alone. We all stand on the shoulders of others to be where we are. Thank you . . .

- Esther Fedorkevich, for believing in me.
- Whitney and all the crew at Fedd Agency, for your personal encouragement.
- Oasis Church members and leaders who pray, support, and encourage me to be who God created me to be.
- Sherryl B., Kenny and Carrie M., for your prayer support.
- Holly, for being my friend, lover, and cheerleader. Thank you for laughing with me, praying with me, listening to me, and understanding my heart. Thank you for being there beside me during the times of celebration *and* the times of struggle. Thank you for letting me finish my own sentences. #Occasionally. Thank you for being my partner in trying to demonstrate that #LoveWorks.
- Jordan and Paris, for believing in and loving your dad. You are an inspiration.
- Laura Barker and the team at WaterBrook, for your patient support on this book.
- Cara Highsmith, for helping me get my words right.
- To the massive company of friends and family that have loved, challenged, and supported me.
- To the leaders and mentors who inspired me, though you may be unaware I was watching.
- Rob Koke, Phil Wright, John Siebeling, Kenneth Ulmer, and Justin Beckett, for being a circle of friends who bring strength to my life.

# Notes

### Chapter 1: Interpreting Your Dreams

1. "Billy Graham: Biography," Bio, www.biography.com/people/billy-graham-9317669.
2. Cecilia Rasmussen, "Billy Graham's Star Was Born at His 1949 Revival in Los Angeles," *Los Angeles Times,* September 2, 2007, http://articles.latimes.com/2007/sep/02/local/me-then2.
3. Matthew 19:26.
4. Colossians 1:9–10, NLT.

### Chapter 2: Your Extraordinary, Ordinary Life

1. See Genesis 1:27.
2. Ephesians 3:20.
3. Luke 16:10.
4. 2 Corinthians 8:12.

### Chapter 3: The Great Exchange

1. Luke 4:5–8.
2. Genesis 37:5–8, NLT.
3. Luke 14:26, CEV.
4. "Biography," John Grisham, www.jgrisham.com/bio.
5. Psalm 105:19–20, NLT.
6. See Genesis 39:2–6.
7. See Matthew 25:21.
8. Psalm 25:4–5.

*Chapter 4: Distractions, Divine Interruptions, and Defining Moments*

1. Ephesians 5:15–16.
2. World Water Council, "Water Crisis," www.worldwatercouncil.org /library/archives/water-crisis.
3. Claire Hajaj, "Children's World Water Forum: Calling for Change," UNICEF, March 17, 2006, www.unicef.org/wash/index_31731 .html.
4. "Why Water?," Generosity.org, http://generosity.org/why-water.
5. There are two organizations: the for-profit company Generosity Water, set up to help raise more funds for our water projects and run by other investors, and the nonprofit Generosity.org.
6. Proverbs 15:22.
7. Matthew 19:14.
8. Jarrod Luciano, "Conan O'Brian [sic] Farewell Speech," YouTube video, June 12, 2013, www.youtube.com/watch?v=QEF_7ROoNeo.

*Chapter 6: Finding Your Way in a Desert*

1. Isaiah 43:18–19, NKJV.
2. Isaiah 35:5–7, NKJV.
3. Proverbs 15:22.
4. Proverbs 17:22, NLT.
5. It doesn't stand for "Bible Study" either.
6. Ephesians 6:17; John 1:14, NLT.

*Chapter 7: Dream Thieves*

1. 1 Samuel 17:45.
2. John 10:10.
3. Harmony Dust Grillo, "Harmony's Story," Treasures, http:// iamatreasure.com/stories/harmonys-story.

4. Treasures, http://iamatreasure.com.

5. "SoulFires: Harmony Star Dust," Treasures, http://iamatreasure.com /wp-content/uploads/2015/09/Treasures_Press_Outreach_2007.pdf.

6. 1 Thessalonians 5:18.

7. Psalm 42:5.

8. Horatio Spafford, "It Is Well with My Soul," public domain.

9. Philippians 4:7, NKJV.

10. Dawn Levy, "George B. Dantzig, Operations Research Professor, Dies at 90," *Stanford News,* May 25, 2005, http://news.stanford.edu /news/2005/may25/dantzigobit-052505.html.

### Chapter 8: Choosing Friends

1. Walt Disney, quoted in Jeff James, "Leadership Lessons from Walt Disney: How to Inspire Your Team," *Talking Point* (blog), Disney Institute, March 27, 2014, https://disneyinstitute.com/blog/2014/03 /leadership-lessons-from-walt-disney-how-to-inspire-your-team/252.

2. Proverbs 27:17, NLT.

3. Admiral William H. McRaven, "Adm. McRaven Urges Graduates to Find Courage to Change the World," UTNews, May 16, 2014, http:// news.utexas.edu/2014/05/16/mcraven-urges-graduates-to-find-courage -to-change-the-world.

4. Matthew 18:20.

5. Jonah 1:12.

6. R. Charli Carpenter, *Born of War: Protecting Children of Sexual Violence Survivors in Conflict Zones* (West Hartford, CT: Kumarian, 2007), 101.

### Chapter 9: The Unwelcome Crisis

1. See John 16:33.

2. 2 Corinthians 4:8–11, 13–18, NLT.

3. L. R. Knost, quoted in Alan D. Wolfelt, *Grief One Day at a Time* (Fort Collins, CO: Companion, 2016), March 1.

4. Psalm 34:18, NLT.

## Chapter 10: Betrayal's Burden

1. See Genesis 37:18–36.

2. Philippians 4:8–9.

3. Hebrews 12:14–15.

4. Corrie ten Boom, *Tramp for the Lord* (New York: Jove, 1974), 54.

5. Ten Boom, *Tramp for the Lord,* 54–55.

6. Luke 22:47–48, NLT.

7. Luke 19:37–38.

8. Luke 23:34, NLT.

## Chapter 11: I'll Have What They're Having

1. Martin Luther, quoted in Aymon de Albatrus, "Martin Luther," www .albatrus.org/english/potpourri/quotes/martin_luther_quotes.htm.

2. 2 Corinthians 10:12.

3. John 21:22, NLT.

4. Psalm 23:1.

## Chapter 12: The Generosity Factor

1. Luke 6:38: "Give, and it will be given to you. A good measure, pressed down, shaken together and running over, will be poured into your lap. For with the measure you use, it will be measured to you."

2. John 3:16.

3. Titus 3:4–6.

4. James 1:5.

5. Matthew 26:10–13, NLT.

6. John 13:35.

7. Public Library of Science, "Empathy and Oxytocin Lead to Greater Generosity," *ScienceDaily,* November 8, 2007, www.sciencedaily.com /releases/2007/11/071107074321.htm. And Kenneth Cloke, "Bringing Oxytocin into the Room: Notes on the Neurophysiology of Conflict," International Mediation Institute, https://imimediation.org/oxytocin _ken_cloke.

8. 2 Corinthians 9:6–8.

9. See Matthew 6:3–4.

10. See Mark 12:41–44.

11. Proverbs 11:25, NLT.

12. See Ephesians 3:20.

13. Versions of this story are widely found online. One source is Alice Smith, "God Owns All the Doughnuts," *Crucible: A Melting Pot* (blog), http://alisssmith.typepad.com/alice_smith/2009/07/we-have -a-saying-in-our-house-god-owns-all-the-donuts.html.

### Chapter 13: Being a Dream-Maker

1. To find out more about this amazing horse, read *Seabiscuit* by Laura Hillenbrand.

2. "Number of Deaths Due to HIV/AIDS," Global Health Observatory, World Health Organization, www.who.int/gho/hiv/epidemic_status /deaths_text/en.

3. "Watoto Villages," Watoto, www.watoto.com/our-work/watoto -villages.

4. See Exodus 2:1–10, ESV. This home has grown so much that there are now two homes for babies: Baby Watoto Suubi in Kampala and Baby Watoto Gulu in Northern Uganda.

5. Chen Si, quoted in Jim Yardley, "On a Bridge of Sighs, the Suicidal Meet a Staying Hand," *New York Times,* September 21, 2004, www

.nytimes.com/2004/09/21/world/asia/on-a-bridge-of-sighs-the-suicidal -meet-a-staying-hand.html.

6. M. R. Phillips, MD, "Suicide and Attempted Suicide—China, 1990– 2002," *Morbidity and Mortality Weekly Report* 53, no. 22 (June 11, 2004), Centers for Disease Control and Prevention, www.cdc.gov /mmwr/preview/mmwrhtml/mm5322a6.htm.

7. Yardley, "On a Bridge of Sighs."

8. Yardley, "On a Bridge of Sighs."

### Chapter 14: When the Heavens Open

1. See 2 Kings 6:8–23.

2. Ken Shulman, "Monumental Toil to Restore the Magnificent," *New York Times,* July 2, 1995, www.nytimes.com/1995/07/02 /arts/art-monumental-toil-to-restore-the-magnificent.html?page wanted=all.

3. See Matthew 17:20.

4. John 3:16.

5. Matthew 3:17.

6. Job 39:21–24.

7. See Mark 5:24–34.

8. Mark 5:28, AMPC.

9. Mark 5:34.

10. Mark 5:31.

11. Proverbs 3:5–6, NLT.

### Chapter 15: If This Were My Last Week on Earth

1. 2 Timothy 4:6-8, MSG.

2. Randy Pausch, "Really Achieving Your Childhood Dreams" (talk, University Lecture Series: Journeys, Carnegie Mellon University,

Pittsburgh, PA, September 18, 2007), www.cs.cmu.edu/~pausch /Randy/pauschlastlecturetranscript.pdf.

3. Sebastien Gendry, "Urban Myth: Children Laugh 300 to 400 Times a Day, and Adults Only 17.5," Laughter Online University, www .laughteronlineuniversity.com/children-laughter-frequency.

4. Norman Cousins, *Anatomy of an Illness: As Perceived by the Patient* (New York: Norton, 1979), 43–44.

5. Matthew 20:26.

6. Andy Stanley, "One, Not Everyone" (sermon), www2.northpoint ministries.org/player/player.jsp?occurrenceID=5579.

7. Stephanie Webber, "Tim McGraw Honors Late Dad, Mets Pitcher Tug McGraw, at World Series Game," *Us Weekly*, November 3, 2015, www.usmagazine.com/celebrity-news/news/tim-mcgraw-honors -late-dad-mets-pitcher-tug-mcgraw-at-world-series--2015311.

8. Isaiah 55:8, NLT.

# About the Author

PHILIP WAGNER is the founding and lead pastor of Oasis Church in Los Angeles and the founder of Generosity.org. Oasis is an innovative and racially diverse church, largely comprised of people in their twenties and thirties. Oasis is known for its local and global outreach to the impoverished, especially orphans and widows, and for funding clean-water projects. Philip and his wife, Holly, started Oasis in 1984 in Beverly Hills with ten people. Today they've grown to more than three thousand members.

Philip is a speaker and humanitarian and has spoken at conferences, seminars, and churches around the world. He inspires people to engage in life's greatest adventure: discovering and reaching God's purpose and dreams for their lives. He also speaks on leadership development.

Philip and Holly cofounded GodChicks and the She Rises annual women's conference, which currently meets at the Dolby Theater in Hollywood.

He is also the author of *The Marriage Makeover* and coauthor, with Holly, of *Love Works*.

Philip and Holly live in Los Angeles and have been married for more than thirty years. They have two grown children, Paris and Jordan.

# Navigate Life's Storms and Discover a Courage Like No Other

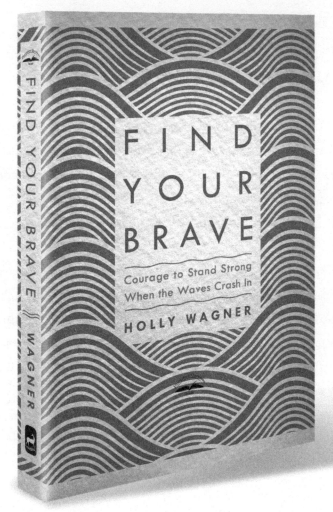

When life's storms thunder and rage, place your trust in the One who still commands the winds and sea. It's time to *Find Your Brave*.

**Start reading now at WaterBrookMultnomah.com!**

#refusetosink      FindYourBraveBook.com       **WATERBROOK**